Cambridge Elements ≣

Elements in Ancient East Asia
edited by
Erica Fox Brindley
Pennsylvania State University
Rowan Kimon Flad
Harvard University

VIOLENCE AND THE RISE OF CENTRALIZED STATES IN EAST ASIA

Mark Edward Lewis
Stanford University

CAMBRIDGE
UNIVERSITY PRESS

CAMBRIDGE
UNIVERSITY PRESS

University Printing House, Cambridge CB2 8BS, United Kingdom

One Liberty Plaza, 20th Floor, New York, NY 10006, USA

477 Williamstown Road, Port Melbourne, VIC 3207, Australia

314–321, 3rd Floor, Plot 3, Splendor Forum, Jasola District Centre,
New Delhi – 110025, India

103 Penang Road, #05–06/07, Visioncrest Commercial, Singapore 238467

Cambridge University Press is part of the University of Cambridge.

It furthers the University's mission by disseminating knowledge in the pursuit of education, learning, and research at the highest international levels of excellence.

www.cambridge.org
Information on this title: www.cambridge.org/9781108972147
DOI: 10.1017/9781108975551

First published 2022

A catalogue record for this publication is available from the British Library.

ISBN 978-1-108-97214-7 Paperback
ISSN 2632-7325 (online)
ISSN 2632-7317 (print)

Violence and the Rise of Centralized States in East Asia

Elements in Ancient East Asia

DOI: 10.1017/9781108975551
First published online: March 2022

Mark Edward Lewis
Stanford University
Author for correspondence: Mark Edward Lewis,

Abstract: Violence, both physical and nonphysical, is central to any society, but it is a version of the problem that it claims to solve. This Element examines how states in ancient East Asia, from the late Shang through the end of the Han dynasty, wielded violence to create and display authority, and also how their licit violence was entangled in the "savage" or "criminal" violence whose suppression justified their power. The East Asian cases are supplemented through citing comparable Western ones. The themes examined include the emergence of the warrior as a human type, the overlap of hunts and combat (and the overlap between treatments of alien species and alien peoples), sacrifice of both alien captives and "death attendants" from one's own groups, the impact of military specialization and the increased scale of armies, the emergent ideal of self-sacrifice, and the diverse aspects of violence in the regime of law.

Keywords: violence, empire, state, China, ancient world

ISBNs: 9781108972147 (PB), 9781108975551 (OC)
ISSNs: 2632-7325 (online), 2632-7317 (print)

Contents

Introduction

Violence, both physical and nonphysical, is central to constructing any society, but it is often problematic in that it is a version of the problem that it sometimes claims to solve. This Element examines how the evolving state orders in ancient East Asia – from the late Shang through the end of the Han dynasty – wielded different forms of violence in their military, political, social, and religious orders to create and display their power, but also shows how their licit forms of violence were entangled in the "savage" or "criminal" violence whose conquest or suppression routinely justified their claims to power. At each stage, the East Asian case will be supplemented through examining comparable cases in the West – for example, "Bronze Age theocracies" of Mesopotamia and Egypt in comparison with the Shang; late Republican Rome in comparison with the Warring States; and late antiquity in comparison with the Han empires. Among the themes examined will be the emergence of the warrior as a human type; the overlap of hunts and combat in early political forms (and the relationship between treatments of alien species and alien peoples); human sacrifice of both alien captives and "death attendants" from one's own group (followers in life who were sacrificed to attend the ruler in death); the impact of military specialization and the increased scale of armies; the role of an ideal of self-sacrifice; how the violence of law (along with lawlike practices including vengeance) was both justified and hidden in order to keep the society functioning; the emergence of political orders based on private armies and resettled, tribal peoples; and the evolving forms of sacrifice as a basis of power.

This dualism of violence as a force that both destroys and preserves order is indicated in many languages. Thus, in early Chinese the standard term for "government" (*zheng *tsyeng*政) was homophonous and graphically identical (before the standardization of significs) with "military offensive" (*zheng *tsyeng* 征) and also with 正 (*zheng *tsyeng*), which as a transitive verb indicated to "correct" or "rectify" – this could also indicate a form of violence (see the next section). Likewise the word *zui *dzwojH* 罪 indicated both a crime and a punishment (although this is in part simply a feature of classical Chinese in which a noun could serve as a putative verb; the fact that in this case the operation is so routine that both senses are common indicates the clear overlap of the two senses). In Latin, the word *vis* "force" was related both to *violare* "to outrage, treat with violence," but also to *vir* "a true man" and hence to *virtus*, the "virtuous potency" which allowed a man to win glory and honor in public service. Similarly, the German *Gewalt* was derived from the old Germanic *waldan*, which meant "to reign, to control," but in later German came to indicate both "violence" and "authority."[1]

---

[1] Willem Schinkel, *Aspects of Violence: A Critical Theory* (New York: Palgrave Macmillan, 2010), pp. 19–21.

Definitions

Most definitions of "violence" focus on the narrow sense of it as *intentional, direct physical harm*. In my book *Sanctioned Violence* this sense was pushed to the extreme of referring to taking life, specifically taking life to create or preserve social order through: (1) forcibly compelling, (2) defining social groups, (3) marking matters of highest significance (for which one would kill or die), and (4) serving in mythic or metaphoric thinking.[2] Many such definitions also list forms of violence, usually with some apology that these are inevitably incomplete, hence leaving a vague definition.[3]

However, some scholars studying violence in recent decades have argued for an "extended" definition that goes beyond wielding physical force to inflict harm. The weaknesses of the "narrow" definition are elaborated by Willem Schinkel.[4] First, even in common speech the term "violence" is applied to structures or forms of conduct that limit people or cause them to "suffer" from diminution of their prospects, even if there is no physical pain.[5] Second, among such nonphysical violence, constraints or abuses imposed upon people through language, within which people are thrust into categories that radically diminish them, are particularly important.[6] Third, narrow definitions routinely insist on the "legitimacy" or "illegitimacy" of violence, which are themselves imposed within the process of some political order defining what does or does not count in this category.[7] Fourth, the narrow definition of violence insists on the presence of an actor or agent, thereby occluding any idea of "structural violence" that is built into the process of maintaining differentiations within the social order but routinely unrecognized because "no agency can be pointed out

---

[2.] Mark Edward Lewis, *Sanctioned Violence in Early China* (Albany: SUNY Press, 1990), pp. 1–5.

[3.] Yves Michaud, *La Violence* (Paris: Presses Universitaires de France, 1986), ch. 1; Xavier Crettiez, *Les formes de la violence* (Paris: La Découverte, 2008), introduction.

[4.] Schinkel, *Aspects of Violence*, p. 35. On pp. 68–82 he lists nine advantages for his extended definition of violence as what contributes to a "reduction of being."

[5.] See Arthur Kleinman, Veena Das, and Margaret Lock, eds., *Social Suffering* (Berkeley: University of California Press, 1997); Veena Das, Arthur Kleinman, Mamphela Ramphele, and Pamela Reynolds, eds., *Violence and Subjectivity* (Berkeley: University of California Press, 2000); Michel Wieviorka, *Violence: A New Approach*, tr. David Macey (Los Angeles: Sage, 2009).

[6.] Among discussions of language as a form of violence, the most influential are those in Pierre Bourdieu's theory of "symbolic violence." See *Ce que parler veut dire* [*Language and Symbolic Power*] (Paris: Fayard, 1982); *La Distinction: critique social du jugement* (Paris: Minuit, 1984), pp. 535–585; *Raisons pratiques: Sur la théorie de l'action* (Paris: Seuil, 1994), ch. 4, 6; *Méditation pascaliennes* (Paris: Seuil, 1997), pp. 10, 92, 98–99, 116, 197–288. See also Schinkel, *Aspects of Violence*, pp. 188–191.

[7.] David Riches, "The Phenomenon of Violence," in *The Anthropology of Violence*, ed. D. Riches (Oxford: Blackwell, 1986), pp. 1–27; the other essays in this volume; and Bettina E. Schmidt and Ingo W. Schroder, eds., *Anthropology of Violence and Conflict* (New York: Routledge, 2001).

as its intentional source."[8] Finally, closely related to the fourth point, narrow definitions of violence focus on violence as an *act*, while obscuring the way that it often works as a protracted, and hence less immediately visible, *process*.

Among the extended theories of violence, the most useful, because its highly abstract nature provides a phenomenological kernel that works through all the others, is Schinkel's assertion that it represents a "reduction of being."[9] Any action or structure that limits or diminishes the capacities or potential of certain people is a form of violence, in this extended sense. For example, violence in the narrow sense against Blacks in the USA would refer to lynching; to murders by police; and to the robberies, assaults, and murders suffered at the hands of criminals in their communities. In Schinkel's extended sense, it would include all the institutions and practices that have impoverished and diminished Blacks: red lining, racial restriction covenants, routine denial of loans, ignoring job applications from people with Black-sounding names (when identical applications with white names result in interviews), exclusion from the benefits of the GI Bill, voter suppression, disproportionate subjection to stop and frisk, disproportionate frequency of arrest and prosecution, disproportionate imprisonment, the "war on drugs," extreme penalties for crack as opposed to powdered cocaine, and so on. It would also, under the rubric of "symbolic violence," include anti-Black discourse that posits their inferior intelligence, limited capacity to experience pain, and other supposed biological differences that justify discrimination.

Schinkel also invokes Wittgenstein's theory of "seeing an aspect," meaning that the speaker "sees something *as* something," without claiming to be exhaustive and uniquely true. Perceiving these phenomena *as* violence means seeing them from a new perspective, and making new connections, without insisting that the concept "violence" exhausts what could be said about them.[10] Schinkel's ideas have been developed by Roderick Campbell into a model of "moral economies" or "regimes" of violence in which different "local worlds" construct their own "hierarchies of being" that exalt certain groups into a higher category of existence, and diminish others to lower forms of being.[11] This improves upon Schinkel in that it emphasizes the dual aspect of creating such hierarchies, both the radical diminution of some (the victims) and the equally

---

[8.] Schinkel, *Aspects of Violence*, pp. 185–189.

[9.] Aspects of this definition and its superiority to rivals are elaborated in Schinkel, *Aspects of Violence*, ch. 1–3.

[10.] Schinkel, *Aspects of Violence*, pp. 5–12. The title of Schinkel's book places this "aspectual" approach at the center of attention.

[11.] Roderick Campbell, "Introduction: Toward a Deep History of Violence and Civilization," *in Violence and Civilization: Studies of Social Violence in History and Prehistory*, ed. Roderick Campbell (Oxford: Oxbow Books, 2014), pp. 6–10, 17–18.

radical inflation of others (the perpetrators). One must also keep in mind that the supposed exaltation or inflation of the condition of the perpetrators of violence often makes sense only within the society or the privileged groups who perform the violence. Thus people celebrated European colonialism as "civilizing" or "spreading law" to supposed savages, while it actually attained hitherto unimagined forms and degrees of cruelty.[12]

Campbell has applied this model to his own studies of Shang violence (see the next section), and I will demonstrate its usefulness in the analysis of later periods. However, I would first like to add the point, which will recur, that as a mode of generating power and status, violence in both the broad and narrow senses remains perpetually dangerous and unstable. This is because it is usually scarcely distinguishable from, or even worse than, what it claims to destroy or suppress (as in the aforementioned case of European colonialism). It consequently remains permanently riven with tensions or contradictions, and ceases to justify any structure of authority in the very moment of its failure, and to justify post facto any new structure imposed.

Violence in the Shang World and Other "Bronze Age Theocracies"

Campbell's recent monograph – *Violence, Kinship and the Early Chinese State: The Shang and their World* (Cambridge, 2018) – has been described by Lothar von Falkenhausen as "the best one-volume treatment of Shang civilization to have come out since K. C. Chang's still useful but out-of-date *Shang Civilization* (New Haven, 1980)." In this book, as the title suggests, the role of violence in defining the Shang world has a prominent place.[13] It argues that the polity based at Shang Anyang was distinguished by the tremendous scale of its violence: warfare, hunting, human sacrifice, other sacrifices, and tens of thousands of real and symbolic weapons that were buried with the dead. At the apogee of this structure was warfare, in which the king moved across his realm and those of clients or allies, securing peace through touring, hunting, gifting, offering sacrifices, and – when necessary – defeating an opponent in battle. The

---

[12] See Adam Hochschild, *King Leopold's Ghost: A Story of Greed, Terror, and Heroism in Colonial Africa* (Boston: Houghton Mifflin, 1998). Nidesh Lawtoo, ed., *Conrad's Heart of Darkness and Contemporary Thought: Revisiting the Horror with Lacoue-Labarthe* (London: Bloomsbury, 2012) contains some of the most perceptive writings on "civilization" and its "darkness" seen through the lens of what has become the classic mythic text of colonialism.

[13] Campbell, *Violence, Kinship, and the Early Chinese State*, "War and Sacrifice in the Second Millennium BCE," pp. 74–84; "Violence and Shang Civilization" (divided into "War, Sacrifice and the Polity" and "The Logic of Sacrifice"), pp. 178–211. See also Campbell, "Transformations of Violence: On Humanity and Inhumanity in Early China," in *Violence and Civilization*, pp. 94–118.

inscriptional material suggests that his exercise of coercive power was "largely personal, direct, and intense, if sporadic and unsystematic." "Resources of violence" were dispersed among many local rulers and lineage heads who engaged in raids, campaigns, and rebellions, forcing the king to constantly negotiate alliances, and resort only when necessary to wars. More distant peoples who were not party to alliances were the target of more overt hostilities, including campaigns apparently fought to secure victims for large-scale human sacrifices. In this way a hierarchy of peoples – ranging from the Shang royal lineage itself, through its followers and allies, to the most distant and alien tribes – was marked out in the different forms of violence to which they could be subjected.

Followers of the Shang king formed kin groups based on shared residence and burial, but also on their role in state violence. Specifically, the units for military action seem to have been these kin groups, the oracle-bone graph for which depicted two men grouped under a banner, suggesting a military origin and role. The routine burial of weapons with these people may also have indicated their function as warriors. Moreover, inscriptions indicate that these lineages also provided the basic terms for defining identity within the Shang polity, with interlineage status based largely on genealogical relationship to the Shang king. All these people made offerings to their own lineage ancestors, but they also joined under the king who, as apex lineage leader, united them in the service of ancestral honor, sacrifices, and wars.[14]

The "hierarchy of being" articulated in the Shang "moral economy of violence" was most detailed in the patterns that culminated in human sacrifice. More broadly, it was embedded in a "hierarchy of ancestral authority" that extended from the lowest creatures, through lesser peoples, members of the Shang state, the elite, the king and his royal ancestors, up to the high god, Di, and associated powers of the land. The aforementioned expeditions and systems of alliance marked the king's claim to the four quarters of the earth, although he relied on the support of his allies. This structure, established in the violence of hunting and wars that pacified the outer realms, led up to the numerous human sacrifices marking royal burials. The combination of excavated tombs and inscriptional materials maps out at least three levels of sacrifice: (1) war captives who were decapitated, burned, or buried alive, and thus reduced to "nameless sacrificial capital"; (2) enemy leaders who were named (and whose function as named trophies marks their higher political status) in divinations on sacrifice, which stipulated to which ancestor they were offered as a trophy for

---

[14.] Campbell, *Violence, Kinship and the Early Chinese State*, ch. 5, esp. pp. 154, 162–163, 174–177.

his glory; and (3) "death attendants" who were buried intact and enjoyed a regular burial, except for being interred in someone else's tomb.[15] These would have been women, attendants, or officials of the deceased who more or less willingly followed their lord in death. The first two categories figured only in the largest tombs – those of the king and his highest allies – which indicates that they marked royal power, while the last type appear in a wider range of tombs. This dispersed ability to command human sacrifice, like the dispersed claim to military resources, shows the distribution of coercive capital through the segmentary structure of lineages that formed the unstable order of the Shang world.

This partial dispersal of military power, marked by the negotiation of alliances and general appearance of "death attendants" in elite tombs, is also indicated by the association of elite status with weapons and symbolic artifacts derived from them since the early third millennium BCE, and the consistent place of weapons as a percentage of grave goods since the second millennium. Indeed, in the Anyang period some elite tombs contained hoards of weapons sufficient to outfit a small army. Thus status and violence seem to have been symbolically intertwined since the third millennium BCE. Moreover, in the late Anyang period this practice seems to have extended even to nonelite tombs, suggesting that a wider range of the burial community could "join their ancestors equipped with what would have been markers of elite status in earlier times."[16]

In summation, Campbell argues that "war and sacrifice were two aspects of the same structuring institution, creating order and a measure of ontological security." Such warfare was not a breakdown of negotiated order, nor a continuation of policy by other means, but an enactment of authority, which gloried in wielding a range of elite insignia including ritual weapons, chariots, and monumental human sacrifice. The internal pacification achieved through Shang warfare was not simply the elimination of all military threats, but a creation of order out of "the anarchic forces of the world." Finally, this should not be understood as a "monopoly" of violence within a "state" order, but rather a set of "hierarchically structuring practices differentially participated in by all." While the Shang king was superior in the scale of the armies he could command and the human sacrifices he could offer up, a range of lesser elites participated in the violent structuring of the world through warfare, hunting, and sacrifice.[17]

---

[15] For a comparative study of "death attendants," focusing on early dynastic Egypt, see Ellen F. Morris, "(Un)Dying Loyalty: Meditations on Retainer Sacrifice in Ancient Egypt and Elsewhere," in Campbell, *Violence and Civilization*, pp. 61–93.

[16] Campbell, *Violence, Kinship and the Early Chinese State*, pp. 76–81.

[17] Campbell, *Violence, Kinship and the Early Chinese State*, pp. 210–211.

This pattern of a polity built around a divinely empowered king who actively wielded violence to shape the world also appeared in other "Bronze Age theocracies" that had emerged earlier in Mesopotamia and Egypt. The most valuable survey of this is William Hamblin's *Warfare in the Ancient Near East to 1600 BC*. In his introduction he states that for the ancient Near Easterners war "was the means by which the gods restored cosmic order through organized violence undertaken in their name by their divinely ordained kings."[18] Hamblin elaborates this theme over 500 pages, tracing the evolving technologies of organized violence, the shifting depiction (both written and visual) of kings and warriors, and the cultic practices, hymns, and laments for destroyed cities, in which are depicted these interactions between the gods, the divinely sanctioned (and sometimes divinized) rulers, and their priests.

This elaboration of the religious forms in which warfare, hunting, and sacrifice were intertwined is also significant in that, without articulating any theory of violence (as, for example, that which creates "hierarchies of being"), Hamblin's monograph elaborates how the performance of violence served to establish ranked structures ascending from a mastered nature, through defeated foes (artistically depicted as piles of corpses or mutilated body parts), through the armies of the conqueror, then the king himself (routinely larger than his soldiers and often dispatching the enemy chieftain with a blow, or enjoying with his queen the spectacle of his foe's head hanging in the garden), and finally the patron gods who made his victory possible. All these themes, and their repeated representation in the visual arts, have also been the subject of specialist monographs.[19]

The ancient Middle East and Western Europe resembled the Shang world in that the divinely ordained ruler as chief warrior emerged from a world in which weapons had for centuries or millennia been status goods (marked in burials),

---

[18.] Hamblin, *Warfare in the Ancient Near East to 1600 BC: Holy Warriors at the Dawn of History* (London: Routledge, 2006), pp. 12–13.

[19.] On Mesopotamia, the most valuable are Zainab Bahrani, *Rituals of War: The Body and Violence in Mesopotamia* (New York: Zone Books, 2008) – which uses ideas from Foucault and Agamben (see the section, "Violence under the Early Empires") to discuss artistic depictions of combat and royal violence – and Leo Bersani and Ulysse Dutoit, *The Forms of Violence: Narrative in Assyrian Art and Modern Culture* (New York: Schocken, 1985). Amelie Kuhrt, *The Ancient Near East c. 3000–330 BC* (London: Routledge, 1995), vol. 1–2, is a comprehensive survey which gives detailed treatments of the interlinking of war, ritual, and political authority. On the early Egyptian palettes depicting the king's violent dispatching of his foes – often with fields of bound and decapitated corpses – see Whitney Davis, *Masking the Blow: The Scene of Representation in Late Prehistoric Egyptian Art* (Berkeley: University of California Press, 1992). Ellen Morris describes these scenes as becoming "emblematic of pharaonic power for nearly 3,000 years." See Morris, "(Un)Dying Loyalty," pp. 63–65. For later Egyptian history, see Uroš Matić, *Body and Frames of War in New Kingdom Egypt: Violent Treatment of Enemies and Prisoners* (Wiesbaden: Harrassowitz, 2019).

and attacks on humans had been a standard practice (as shown by the evidence of wounds and the mutilation of corpses). The most valuable study of this theme was coauthored by an archaeologist and a doctor/paleopathologist who combined their specialist expertise to trace the evolving social role of violence in prehistory, culminating with the ideological construction of the ideal of the warrior and the hero.[20] This repeated use of funerary ritual to demonstrate the creation of power also shows how humanity has always defined itself in its relations to death, to the extent that some scholars use the appearance of death ritual as a marker of the separation of the human from an animal background, but that these rituals from the beginning served to perpetuate, or extend into the afterlife, power generated through violence.[21]

What this and related works indicate is that small-scale, organized violence in which most males participated was widespread, if not universal, among hunter-gatherers.[22] However, such violence gradually became the sphere of specialists, who wielded their mastery of violence to establish themselves above their erstwhile peers. At some point, through the assimilation of such men into temple-based religions that elevated their chief above all other people, the figure of the king emerged. This may have been linked to the emergence of the idea of sacrifice, as the violence of the hunt (in societies where hunting was no longer the standard mode of attaining food but rather a form of privilege) or that of intercommunal combat was rendered significant or even divine through ritual performances. Some theories have also found in the emergence of sacrificial cults traces of a period when men were as frequently the prey of animals as their hunters.[23]

---

[20]. Jean Guilaine and Jean Zammit, *Le Sentier de la guerre: Visages de la violence préhistorique* (Paris: Seuil, 2001), translated into English as *The Origins of War: Violence in Prehistory* (Oxford: Blackwell, 2005). See also Arther Ferrill, *The Origins of War: From the Stone Age to Alexander the Great* (London: Thames and Hudson, 1985), ch. 1–3; John Carman and Anthony Harding, eds., *Ancient Warfare: Archaeological Perspectives* (Stroud, UK: The History Press, 2009); Bruce Lincoln, *Religion, Empire, and Torture: The Case of Achaemenian Persia, with a Postscript on Abu Ghraib* (Chicago: University of Chicago Press, 2007).

[21]. Jean-Pierre Mohen, *Les Rites de l'au-delà* (Paris: Odile Jacob, 2010), begins by studying the emotions evoked by death, and the use of death ritual to confront these, but then devotes most of his work to showing how the full panoply of warriors, emperors, god-kings, and medieval monarchs perpetuated their status in funerary ritual, often like the Shang kings, using rites that diminished those around them.

[22]. The now classic treatment of this is Lawrence H. Keeley, *War before Civilization: The Myth of the Peaceful Savage* (Oxford: Oxford University Press, 1996). This work is elaborated in Azar Gat, *War in Human Civilization* (Oxford: Oxford University Press, 2006), Part 1. Gat, curiously, does not perceive the rise of specialized violence as a significant development, instead treating state-based violence as a direct extension of the earlier tribal form.

[23]. A useful popularization of this is Barbara Ehrenreich, *Blood Rites: Origins and History of the Passions of War* (New York: Metropolitan Books, 1997), ch. 3–5. The most influential scholarly discussion is Walter Burkert, *Homo Necans: The Anthropology of Ancient Greek Sacrificial*

A classic articulation of the idea that religion and specialized violence (along with some economic capacity) fused in the city to produce monarchy is Lewis Mumford's *The City in History*. He argues that three defining functions of the city – sanctuary, village, and citadel – all existed prior to the city itself, but that these three fused and transfigured one another when brought together behind walls under the authority of a transformed hunting class led by a sacralized monarch. This walled-in settlement then became a "pressure cooker" where the intermingling of people allowed for constant innovation and the increasing specialization that formed self-styled civilizations.[24]

Several scholars have argued that this emergence of specialist warriors and monarchs was linked with the development of agriculture, that the emerging cities made possible by the Neolithic revolution provided the matrix for these developments, and perhaps that it was in the larger cities – where rulers relied on officials to measure taxable harvests and soldiers to enforce collection – that autocracy became possible. As states emerged around these cities, smaller tribal units in the hinterlands still violently defended their autonomy. This model of hunter-gatherers fighting to survive as warrior tribes of relatively equal *male* fighters in a world of expanding states with clear political hierarchies was articulated in articles by the anthropologist Pierre Clastres based on his studies in South America.[25]

The model of tribal resistance to state power is also elaborated by James C. Scott in two books. First, *The Art of Not Being Governed* examined the history of the hill peoples of Southeast Asia who resisted incorporation into the state societies around them. This resistance was based on practices that maintained mobility and fluidity as tribal groups: (1) remaining dispersed in rugged terrain, (2) using cropping practices that allowed mobility, (3) maintaining fluid ethnic identities, (4) following prophetic, millenarian leaders, and (5) keeping

---

Ritual and Myth (Berkeley: University of California Press, 1983). This is summarized in "The Problem of Ritual Killing," in *Violent Origins: Walter Burkert, René Girard and Jonathan Z. Smith on Ritual Killing and Cultural Formation*, ed. R. G. Hamerton-Kelly (Stanford: Stanford University Press, 1987), pp. 149–188. See also Philippe Descola, "Des Proies bien-veillantes: Le Traitement du gibier dans la chasse amazonienne"; Florence Burgat, "La Logique de légitimation de la violence: Animalité vs. Humanité"; and Lucien Scubla, "Ceci n'est pas un meurtre: Ou comment le sacrifice contient la violence," in *De la violence II*, ed. Françoise Héritier (Paris: Odile Jacob, 2005), pp. 19–44, 45–62, and 135–170.

[24.] Lewis Mumford, *The City in History: Its Origins, Its Transformations, and Its Prospects* (New York: MJF Books, 1961), ch. 1–2.

[25.] Pierre Clastres, *La Société contre l'état* (Paris: Minuit, 1974) and *Recherches d'anthropologie politique* (Paris: Seuil, 1980). The former was translated as *Society Against the State: The Leader as Servant and the Humane Uses of Power Among the Indians of the Americas* (New York: Urizen, 1977) and the latter as *Archeology of Violence* (New York: Semiotext(e), 1994). The last two essays in this volume give the best presentation of Clastres's model. On one aspect of this theory, see Severin Fowles, "On Torture in Societies Against the State," in *Violence and Civilization*, pp. 155–163.

a primarily oral culture that allowed them to reinvent their histories and genealogies as they moved between the states. Second, *Against the Grain* traced a similar set of practices among peoples who resisted incorporation into sedentary polities at the time of the introduction of agriculture. Seeking to avoid the crowding, diseases, forced labor, and tyrannical rulers created through the adoption of plow agriculture and settling in cities, such peoples retreated as tribes to the peripheries where they were reconceived as "barbarians." These people, who would roughly correspond to the Qiang and other groups hunted and sacrificed by the Shang kings (indeed, Campbell argues that the word "Qiang" may have come to function as a more general rubric meaning "captive" or "slave"), sometimes maintained themselves in smaller tribes, sometimes were forced into the cities (perhaps to maintain urban populations constantly reduced by the new diseases created through crowding with animals), and sometimes were pressed into forming larger units to resist, units that could themselves destroy their state rivals.[26]

The East Asian pattern of political violence under the subsequent Western Zhou is unclear, because neither their capital nor any royal tombs have been excavated. However, we know that the Zhou had participated in the Shang state as an allied lineage, had at some point withdrawn, and had then emerged to reassert their power through military conquest. While their practice of establishing related lineages and allies in walled settlements distributed across conquered territories seems to have differed from the Shang, the building of the state as a confederation of warrior lineages, with the king predominant through having a more powerful army and supremacy in the sacrificial hierarchy, suggest the carrying forward of the principles that had guided the Shang. Moreover, excavated Western Zhou tombs show similar patterns of human sacrifice. Indeed, although human sacrifice declined after the twelfth century BCE, and critiques of the practice became prominent in the Eastern Zhou, it continued until the emergence of the empire and even increased in the late Warring States period.[27] Nevertheless, by the Eastern Zhou the pattern of

---

[26]. James C. Scott, *The Art of Not Being Governed: An Anarchist History of Upland Southeast Asia* (New Haven: Yale University Press, 2009) and *Against the Grain: A Deep History of the Earliest States* (New Haven: Yale University Press, 2017). The model of the size of cities shaping the emergence of autocracy is articulated in David Stasavage, *The Decline and Rise of Democracy: A Global History from Antiquity to Today* (Princeton: Princeton University Press, 2020). Hamblin's volume already cited shows how "peripheral" peoples or "highlanders" were targets of conquest who sometimes (e.g., Akkadians, Persians) became conquerors. See *Warfare in the Ancient Near East*, pp. 6, 30, 71–72, 81, 84, 100, 109–111, 116–119, 156, 159, 213. For Campbell on the various possible meanings of "Qiang," see *Violence, Kinship and the Early Chinese State*, pp. 205–207.

[27]. Huang Zhanyue 黄展岳, *Gudai rensheng renxun tonglun* 古代人牲人殉通論 (Beijing: Wenwu, 2004); Campbell, "Transformations of Violence," pp. 103–109.

normative, political violence had clearly changed, with human sacrifice assuming a peripheral role. The warrior elite also became a more clearly defined aristocracy practicing primogeniture within cadet lineages that were ranked through genealogical ties to the royal line.

Violence in the Eastern Zhou: Spring and Autumn through the Warring States

The primary change between the Western Zhou and the Eastern was the decline of royal power. This had begun in the tenth century BCE, with the annihilation of the royal army and death of the monarch in King Zhao's disastrous southern expedition, followed by decades of continued decline under King Mu. It culminated with the sack of the capital in 771 BCE, eastward flight, and the loss of the Wei River valley that had been the basis of royal power. The successor states were dominated by a warrior aristocracy that defined itself through warfare, ceremonial hunts, and elaborate sacrifices to ancestral spirits and gods of nature. These all revolved around the service of the state altars, where in addition to sacrifices were offered up prey taken in hunts, booty taken in battle, and the left ears of slain enemies. This situation was summarized by the formula that the nobles were identified through the "great services" of the state: warfare and sacrifice.[28]

This Eastern Zhou pattern of violence carried forward the Shang (and probably Western Zhou) pattern in that it structured a "hierarchy of being" in which the elite was an armed group who engaged in regular warfare, hunts, and sacrifices, from which lower levels of the population were excluded. The changes were the absence of a supreme ruler (with a radically weakened monarchy), a clearer distinction between the warrior nobility and commoners (although this might reflect better documentation, the division between the urban elite and rural peasantry created by the Zhou system suggests a clearer separation), and the relative unimportance of human sacrifice in marking the lowest levels of humanity. Also, as will be discussed later, the warrior nobility was internally ranked through two competing hierarchies. One emphasized their aspect as "nobles," with rankings based on status of lineage, rank of mother, and age. The second emphasized their "warrior" aspect, with status earned through individual heroism in battle, success in interlineage feuds, and the wielding of vengeance. Over the course of the Eastern Zhou the latter hierarchy became more prominent, so the nobles' "hierarchy of being" gradually mutated into the Warring States pattern.

[28.] This summarizes Lewis, *Sanctioned Violence*, ch. 1.

As just touched on, the Eastern Zhou aristocracy was distributed in urban settlements across the Zhou realm, with each cadet lineage reproducing itself through primogeniture. As long as land was available, they settled their cadet lineages in cities with courts that were lesser replicas of the senior lines with ancestral temples, altars of the soil, dependent populations, and military forces. This "segmentary" pattern gave each lineage a base of power largely independent of its titular lord. Along with the fact that all nobles were kin, this led to the lower levels of the nobility enjoying a proximity of status and a casual sociability with their rulers. They also competed with putative superiors in a struggle for honor, wherein the violent "services" that distinguished the nobility were justified as means of gaining glory for the lineage and the self. This was true not only in interstate wars, but also in struggles between lineages within a state, and in vendettas and acts of vengeance. This pursuit of honor through violent competition led to wars of ever-increasing intensity that culminated in the destruction of much of the nobility, and the gradual replacement of noble arms by the mass peasant infantry of the Warring States period.

Hunting no longer served to provide food (although nobles were occasionally described as "meat eaters"), but demarcated social status. Thus nobles were urged to take in the hunt only creatures that would be offered at the ancestral temple, or decorate the implements of warfare and ritual. In this way the hunt "fed" the elevated status of the nobility. Assemblies for hunts also clarified the hierarchical structure fixed by ascribed status:

> Every three years we marshal the troops . . . We display the ornamental patterns [of uniforms, chariots, and banners]; make clear the hierarchy of noble and base [*gui jian* 貴賤]; distinguish ranks [*deng lie* 等列]; order them by age [*shao zhang* 少長]; and rehearse their awesome bearing [*wei yi* 威儀].[29]

This lays out the elite as a military force structured according to ascriptive status, office, and age, depicting a world structured by heredity, where honor and office are tied to one's ranking in the kin structure. An earlier passage also shows how ascriptive status was based on kinship as defined through a combination of age and the status of one's mother:

> Ducal Son Zhouxu was the son of a favorite [concubine of Lord Zhuang of Wey]. He had the lord's favor and was fond of weapons, but the lord did not restrain him. [The lord's wife] Zhuang Jiang [who had an adopted son] hated him. Shi Que remonstrated, "I have heard that if you love a son, you instruct

---

29. *Zuo zhuan zhu* 左傳注, annotated by Yang Bojun 楊伯峻 (Beijing: Zhonghua, 1981), Lord Yin year 5, p. 43. The ideas in this section are discussed in more detail in Mark Edward Lewis, *Honor and Shame in Early China* (Cambridge: Cambridge University Press, 2021), pp. 20–26.

him in duty and do not let him stray into deviance ... If you are going to establish Zhouxu as heir, then settle it now. If you have not decided, then this will be the source of calamity. There are very few who will not grow arrogant when favored, becoming arrogant will be able to accept demotion, being demoted will not become indignant, becoming indignant will be able to keep within proper bounds. Moreover, for the base to block the noble, the younger to insult the elder, the distant to come between kin, the newer to come between those with old ties, the smaller to be placed on top of the greater, or the lewd to destroy the dutiful, these are the six inversions.[30]

The principles of succession are articulated in terms of honorable status (as son of the legitimate wife and of a nobler mother), age, closeness of relationship, established position, and dutifulness. The issue here of the status of mothers shows how women played a crucial role in the calculation of kin-based status, just as they did in the establishment of interstate alliances through marriages.[31]

While seasonal hunts and military training rituals rehearsed the established hierarchy, war was the realm of its potential contestation. Thus, in debates over the conduct of war, some men invoked the model of the state structured, as just described, by ascriptive kin status, while others insisted that it was an arena in which individual or group heroism determined status. This meant that status based on seniority and honor based on valor were in constant tension within the army. As an example of the former position, in the campaign that culminated in the battle of Bi (597 BCE), the chief minister of Jin, Fan Hui, argued that the army should not fight Chu, because the latter was harmonious and well-governed:

> The hundred officers act according to the insignia on their banners and standards [which indicate their ranks and posts]. Without special orders, the military regimen is completely prepared, because they can use their established statutes. When the ruler promotes those of his own clan he selects from close kin, and among those from other clans he selects from old families with

---

[30]. *Zuo zhuan zhu*, Lord Yin year 3, pp. 31–32. On the danger of receiving undue honor, see also Lord Xiang year 24, pp. 1093–1094.

[31]. On political marriages, marital alliances, and affinal relatives in the Spring and Autumn period, see Marcel Granet, *La Polygynie sororale et le sororat dans la Chine féodale: Étude sur les formes anciennes de la polygamie chinoise* (Paris: Leroux, 1920); Melvin P. Thatcher, "Marriages of the Ruling Elite in the Spring and Autumn Period," *in Marriage and Inequality in Chinese Society*, ed. Rubie S. Watson and Patricia B. Ebrey (Berkeley: University of California Press, 1991), pp. 25–57; Kai Vogelsang, "Mit den Waffen der Frauen: Allianzen und Mésallianzen in der Chun qiu-Zeit," in *Die Frau im Alten China: Bild und Wirklichkeit*, ed. Dennis Shilling and Jianfei Kralle (Stuttgart: Steiner, 2001), pp. 1–23; Xu Jieling 徐傑令, *Chunqiu bangjiao yanjiu* 春秋邦交研究 (Beijing: Zhongguo Shehui Kexue, 2004), pp. 198–221; Xu, "Chunqiu shiqi lianyin dui bangjiao yingxiang 春秋時期聯姻對邦交影響," *Dongbei Shida Xuebao* (Zhexue Shehui Kexue Ban), 2004.1, pp. 56–62. For earlier periods, see Maria Khayutina, "Marital Alliances and Affinal Relatives (*Sheng* and *Hungou*) in the Society and Politics of Zhou China in the Light of Bronze Inscriptions," *Early China* 37 (2014), pp. 39–99.

hereditary posts. In promoting men he overlooks none of virtue, and in granting rewards he does not overlook those who toiled ... The nobles and commoners have distinctive patterns on their regalia. The noble [*gui* 貴] are constantly honored [*zun* 尊] and even the base [*jian* 賤, perhaps the lowest nobles, perhaps the "men of the capital"] have graded degrees of awesomeness.[32]

This depicts a well-ordered state where within the army pride of place was ascribed to status based on kinship and seniority. Status structured where each man was placed, what he wore, how he moved, and thus embodied the order that determined victory.

In response, a Jin noble, Xian Hu, presented a radically different vision of honor and the reasons for choosing whether to fight:

Jin became hegemon because of the martial prowess of its armies and the exertions of its officers. Now to lose the allegiance of the regional lords [i.e., lose the hegemony] cannot be called exertion; to have an enemy and not pursue him cannot be called prowess. Rather than being responsible for losing the hegemony, it would be better to die. To assemble an army and set forth, only to retreat on learning that the enemy is strong, is not manly. To receive the charge to command the army and end by losing one's manhood, perhaps the rest of you can do this, but I cannot.

He led his own men to fight, which drew the rest of the army into a major defeat. Although the speech refers to preserving the hegemony, it emphasizes proving the martial prowess and manliness of the Jin nobles, particularly the speaker. This speech and action – which the authors of the *Zuo zhuan* condemn, and for which Xian Hu and his entire lineage were executed – invoked a vision of honor based on individual heroism rather than ascriptive status.[33] Other passages also insist on the necessity of fighting to preserve one's honor.[34]

This emphasis on individual valor, sometimes at the expense of the army, also figures in accounts of the provocations (*zhi shi* 致師) prior to some battles. These were feats of bravado in which one or two chariots rode out and attacked members of the opposing army. Passages refer to seeking permission, but those who were refused sometimes attacked on their own accord. Others engaging in a provocation, shot a deer that was offered as a gift to opponents, leading them to call off pursuit even though battle had already begun.[35] This also shows the pursuit of individual status superseding devotion to the established order.

---

[32] *Zuo zhuan zhu*, Lord Xuan year 12, pp. 724–725.

[33] *Zuo zhuan zhu*, Lord Xuan year 13, p. 752.

[34] *Zuo zhuan zhu*, Lord Xuan year 12, p. 726; Lord Cheng year 16, p. 882; Lord Xiang year 3, p. 929; Lord Zhao year 13, pp. 1353, 1356.

[35] *Zuo zhuan zhu*, Lord Xi year 33, p. 499; Lord Xuan year 12, pp. 734–736; Lord Xuan year 14, p. 752; Lord Cheng year 3, pp. 813–814. Gifts of deer within provocations are on pp. 735, 736.

Another version of using interstate war to defend personal honor figures in the case of Xi Ke of Jin. He desired to avenge an insult suffered on a mission to Qi, but his ruler refused to go to war. However, when the chief minister of Jin, Fan Hui, retired and was replaced by Xi Ke, the latter proceeded to invade Qi over the ruler's objections. While Fan Hui condemned Xi Ke's conduct, the account shows the latter gaining the support of his fellow commanders, conducting himself heroically when wounded in battle, and attributing his victory to the ruler and his fellows.[36] Such stories show how the violence of combat was not controlled by the state, but was regularly translated into struggles of individuals to secure their own glory. This resembles Thucydides's accounts of how in war demagogues subverted the state's interests to increase their own status, as in Cleon's ruining the chance for peace in 425 BCE after Athens's victory at Sphacteria.[37]

Xi Ke's victory at An (589 BCE) also resulted in promoting several men who had distinguished themselves by heroism:

> In the twelfth month, on the *jiaxu* day [26], Jin created the six armies. Han Jue, Zhao Kuo, Shi Zhuangbo, Han Chuan, Xun Zhui, and Zhao Zhan all became ministers as reward for their merit in the victory at An.[38]

Jin previously had three armies, so this doubled its military. Each army had a commander and a second-in-command, so these six received shared command of the new armies. This was notable in two ways. First, it anticipates developments in the Warring States period, leading some scholars to suggest it is a backward projection. However, these expanded armies *do* figure in subsequent Jin victories at Masui (578 BCE) and Yanling (575 BCE).[39] This creation of new ministers with military power continued Jin's path towards dismemberment in the fifth century.

Second, several men honored here for their heroism had also served at the defeat of Bi, where they had pursued personal glory at the expense of the army. Thus Zhao Kuo supported Xian Hu, arguing that the purpose of the campaign was to seek out a foe whom they were now obliged to fight, and if victorious they would gain a domain. Zhao Zhan had led his men to attack the Chu army despite being refused permission to perform a provocation, and was frustrated at not having been made a minister.[40] Thus the expansion of the army rewarded

---

[36.] *Zuo zhuan zhu*, Lord Xuan years 17–18, pp. 771–777; Lord Cheng year 2, pp. 789–796. Xi Ke's heroism is described on pp. 791–792. The sharing of glory (*ming* 明) is discussed on Lord Cheng year 2, p. 806.

[37.] Donald Kagan, *The Archidamian War* (Ithaca: Cornell University Press, 1974), ch. 8.

[38.] *Zuo zhuan zhu*, Lord Cheng year 3, p. 815.

[39.] *Zuo zhuan zhu*, Lord Cheng year 13, pp. 865–866; Lord Cheng year 16, pp. 884–890.

[40.] *Zuo zhuan zhu*, Lord Xuan year 12, pp. 732, 736–738.

men who had previously jeopardized Jin forces in displaying personal courage. This suggests that in the Spring and Autumn period, the organization of the army, which initially had reiterated ascribed status, increasingly became an arena for restructuring the political order to honor individual heroism.

This contradiction between an ascriptive honor defined by the kin system and an individual honor pursued through heroism also figures in discussions of the honor that defined the ruler, and that which marked the highest individual achievement. As for the former, in addition to the passages where being a ruler was justified by the status of one's mother and age in relation to other possible heirs, others justified someone becoming ruler because his virtuous power gained the support of the spirits, the most talented political actors, and the common people. The leading example is Chong'er, who as Lord Wen of Jin became hegemon and is probably the most celebrated ruler in the *Zuo zhuan*.[41] As for the latter, stories speak of certain individuals "completing their fame/ honor [*cheng ming* 成名]" by killing the ruler or expelling him from the state. While such fame is sometimes problematic, being called "bad [*e* 惡]," such stories show how the ideal of winning honor through violence could culminate in justifying treason.[42]

This tension between political hierarchy and martial valor – between the ruler and the hero – is central in ancient Greece and Rome as well as East Asia. In both cultures the hero, through a willingness to die young, sought supreme glory. By embracing death in the name of honor (gained through defying the king), Achilles jeopardized his own army, but thereby won undying glory. Alternatively, young men's need to win honor through heroism could be institutionalized, as in the early Roman practice of allowing individual combat only when permitted by a superior, but placing the youngest men in the front line of the manipular legion where they could display their valor.[43]

[41.] Lewis, *Honor and Shame*, pp. 28–30. For the stories of Chong'er, see Burton Watson, tr., *The Tso Chuan: Selections from China's Oldest Narrative History* (New York: Columbia University Press, 1989), pp. 21–26, 40–66. On his followers helping attain the hegemony, see Wai-yee Li, *The Readability of the Past* (Cambridge, MA: Harvard University Press, 2007), pp. 254–275. On stories of Chong'er as an early romance, see Maria Khayutina, "Die Geschichte der Irrfahrt des prinzen Chong'er und ihre Botschaft," in *Kritik in alten und modernen China*, ed. Heiner Roetz (Wiesbaden: Harrassowitz, 2006), pp. 20–47.

[42.] Lewis, *Honor and Shame*, pp. 40–41.

[43.] J. E. Lendon, *Soldiers and Ghosts: A History of Battle in Classical Antiquity* (New Haven: Yale, 2005), ch. 8. On the "choice of Achilles" to die young for eternal fame, see J.-P. Vernant, Introduction, in *La Mort, les morts dans les sociétés anciennes*, ed. G. Gnoli and J.-P. Vernant (Cambridge: Cambridge University Press, 1982), esp. pp. 12–13; Gregory Nagy, *The Best of the Achaeans: Concepts of the Hero in Archaic Greek Poetry* (Baltimore: Johns Hopkins University Press, 1979); James M. Redfield, *Nature and Culture in the Iliad: The Tragedy of Hector* (Chicago: University of Chicago Press, 1975), pp. 99–109.

The *Iliad*'s theme of the young warrior as the best man served both as a model for later warriors who sought (both in literature and reality) to emulate Achilles. The pursuit of honor, with that of the *polis* and of the individual sometimes coming into conflict and even leading to civil war, is central in Thucydides's *Peloponnesian War*. In more recent times the *klepht* bandits of highland Greece under the Ottoman Empire patterned themselves on their epic ancestors, but followed Hector rather than Achilles, because they remained tied to their native villages. Their life of war and vengeance also copied the Homeric heroes by becoming the theme of ballads immortalizing their honor.[44] Even those who remained in the villages were also "devoted to honor [*philotimos*]," a term based on the word for "honor [*tīmē*]" employed in the epics.[45]

To return to the *Zuo zhuan*, fixing the state's hierarchy in the assembled army also figured in the introduction of legal codes, anticipating developments in the Warring States era and the early empires that will be discussed later.[46] In 621 BCE, when Jin staged its great military review, the man in charge changed the site of the review, reduced the number of armies from five to three, and promoted Zhao Dun to be commander of the central army and thus head of the government. Zhao Dun then reformed Jin's government at the review:

> He established regulations for official service, rectified the application of laws to crimes, put in order litigation proceedings, regulated the conduct of legal proceedings, set right the issue of absconding, fixed adherence to bonds and contracts, corrected outdated practices, firmly grounded the rituals pertaining to rank, restored customary offices, and promoted those who had been blocked and kept in obscurity.[47]

Apart from its emphasis on legal proceedings and their reliance on writing, this reform at the military review is notable for – while recognizing ascriptive

---

[44.] John Campbell, "The Greek Hero," in *Honor and Grace in Anthropology*, ed. J. G. Peristiany and Julian Pitt-Rivers (Cambridge: Cambridge University Press, 1992), pp. 129–149. The Homeric precedent is discussed on pp. 129–134.

[45.] J. K. Campbell, "Honour and the Devil," *in Honour and Shame: The Values of Mediterranean Society*, ed. J. G. Peristiany (London: Weidenfield and Nicolson, 1965), pp. 143, 147, 150–151, 170 n. 6; Peristiany, "Honour and Shame in a Cypriot Highland Village," in *Honour and Shame*, pp. 177, 178–179, 181, 182, 183–187, 189. On *tīmē* in the Homeric epics and in ancient Greece, see Redfield, *Nature and Culture in the Iliad*, pp. 33, 230 n. 13; Nagy, *Best of the Achaeans*, pp. 72–73, 79–80, 82, 94, 114, 118, 119, 125, 131–134, 142, 149–152, 181, 184, 186–188, 215–218, 265–267, 269, 285, 287, 334; A. W. H. Adkins, *Moral Values and Political Behavior in Ancient Greece from Homer to the End of the Fifth Century* (New York, W. W. Norton, 1972), pp. 14–21, 22, 62–64; Peter Brown, *The Making of Late Antiquity* (Cambridge, MA: Harvard University Press, 1978), pp. 31–34.

[46.] Ernest Caldwell, *Writing Chinese Laws: The Form and Function of Legal Statutes Found in the Qin Shuihudi Corpus* (London: Routledge, 2018), ch. 2; Caldwell, "Social Change and Written Law in Early Chinese Legal Thought," *Law and History Review* 32.1 (2014), pp. 1–30.

[47.] *Zuo zhuan zhu*, Lord Wen year 6, pp. 545–546.

status (in referring to "customary" offices and to rituals fixing the social hierarchy) – emphasizing punishing and pursuing recalcitrant elements of the lower population, and promoting and honoring "new" men whose merits surpassed their received status (like Zhao Dun). This indicates how states' increased reliance on legal codes, which with their mutilating punishments were also a form of violence, was fundamental to the gradual replacement of the nobility's old pattern of ascriptive status based on kinship to structuring a state through rewarding service.

Assembling the army was again linked to legal reforms in 513 BCE. Two Jin nobles led out the army and levied a measure of iron, which they used to cast a penal code compiled by Fan Xuanzi. This elicited a "prophecy" attributed to Confucius that Jin would perish because its rulers had cast penal laws into tripods, thus making them public and universally applicable:

> Confucius said, "Jin will perish! It has abandoned all proper degree. It should be guided by the models of degree and measure that [its founder] Tang Shu received from the Zhou king to provide guidelines for governing its people. The hereditary officials preserved this by observing their hierarchy, and consequently the people could honor their nobles, and the nobles maintain their hereditary duties [*ye* 業]. Noble and base did not deviate from these, which is why we call them 'proper degree.' Thereby Lord Wen created the office of keeper of ranks, set up the legal code at the army's muster at Pilu, and became hegemon. Now they abandon such degree and create 'punishment tripods,' so the people attend only to the tripods. How can they honor the nobles? How can the nobles preserve their hereditary duties? If the noble and base lack all order, how can one manage a domain? Moreover, Fan Xuanzi's legal code derives from the army's muster at Yi [referring to Zhao Dun's code], a period of disorder in Jin. How can it provide a legal norm?"[48]

The ultimate crime of the tripods was to undercut the order based on noble honor in the name of a universalizing justice that rewarded those who provided service. Moreover, epitomizing the sphere of the nobles as *ye* – which combined duties, work, and inheritance – emphasized the hereditary aspect of nobility and the honor that had defined Jin, but which now was being abandoned through the imposition of legal codes within the army. Finally, the idea attributed to Confucius that Lord Wen attained the hegemony by structuring honor within the army's ranks reiterates the model in which political order depended on ascriptive status physically enacted in the army. However, the anecdote indicates that this older model was being abandoned, while condemning the innovation.

---

[48] *Zuo zhuan zhu*, Lord Zhao year 29, p. 1504. On the laws drafted by Fan Xuanzi, see Lord Wen year 6, p. 545. On Lord Wen's assembling the army at Pilu, see Lord Xi year 27, p. 447.

Most modern discussions of "Confucius's" speech focus on the line about "attending only to the tripods."[49] They sometimes cite a letter from Shuxiang criticizing an earlier casting of laws by Zichan in the state of Zheng. This letter describes an imaginary early state based on what would become the highest "classicist" virtues, argues that introducing written laws destroyed this ideal order by making people disputatious, and concludes that each of the ancient Three Dynasties had introduced written penal laws in their decline. Finally, it links the casting of law on tripods with other Warring States reforms, and predicts the destruction of Zheng.[50] As a document it appears anachronistic and is less valuable than "Confucius's" critique. Whereas the latter expresses the values and practices of the nobility as portrayed in the *Zuo zhuan*, "Shuxiang's" antiquity guided by ethical virtues resembles the fantasy of a Warring States scholar. Moreover, the *Zuo zhuan* clearly sides with Zichan, whose descendants flourished in Zheng, while Shuxiang's lineage was eliminated shortly after his death.

Notably, Confucius elsewhere praises Shuxiang for ruthless impartiality in carrying out the law, even executing his own kinsman. This is described as "correctly carrying out the penal writings [*zheng xing shu* 正刑書, presumably referring to the penal laws drafted in 621 BCE]" and expressing "the lingering influence of ancient fairness [*gu zhi yi zhi* 古之遺直]." Confucius even states that Shuxiang, in executing his own kin, "increased his glory [*yi rong* 益榮]."[51] Thus Confucius praises Shuxiang for doing what his supposed letter condemns, and justifies this in terms of a vision of antiquity that contradicts the letter. Only in "Confucius's" argument can we see the true background to the emergence of formal legal systems as an aspect of the changing nature of the army based on rewarding individual heroism.

A further Spring and Autumn innovation in using violence to mobilize and rank humanity through evolving forms of legality was the emergence of the "blood covenant." In this ceremony the blood of a sacrificial animal was applied to the mouths of those who swore an oath of loyalty, and then smeared on written copies of the oath that were buried to bring them to the attention of

---

[49.] The casting of these tripods is cited in modern studies of Chinese law as evidence of the earliest legal "code." See Derk Bodde and Clarence Morris, *Law in Imperial China: Exemplified by 190 Ch'ing Dynasty Cases Translated from the Hsing-an hui-lan* (Philadelphia: University of Pennsylvania Press, 1967), pp. 15–17; R. P. Peerenboom, *Law and Morality in Ancient China: The Silk Manuscripts of Huang-Lao* (Albany: SUNY Press, 1993), pp. 135–137; Yongping Liu, *Origins of Chinese Law: Penal and Administrative Early Development* (Oxford: Oxford University Press, 1998), pp. 52–53. The accounts of earlier laws from Lord Wen and Zhao Dun indicate that this argument is not accurate, and that the casting of the tripod was part of an extended development.

[50.] *Zuo zhuan zhu*, Lord Zhao year 6, pp. 1274–77.

[51.] *Zuo zhuan zhu*, Lord Zhao year 14, p. 1367.

chthonic deities. First used by the most powerful of the Eastern Zhou states to forge leagues and impose their authority as "master of the covenant," these oaths gradually came to be employed whenever men forged new coalitions or imposed binding ties on their followers. They were even employed to organize conspiracies, insurrections, and civil wars. Such covenants drew new social elements, most notably the "capital populace," into political struggles. As civil wars and the increasingly frequent destruction of states and lineages tore apart the old order, blood covenants became crucial as the primary means of binding men together for action, distinguishing and ranking those who were politically active, and thus providing the foundation for the legal codes that came to define political authority in the late Spring and Autumn period.

The developments again demonstrate the contradictions inherent in using violence to create a political (or religious) order. On the one hand, performing violence was the defining attribute of nobles; the capacity to battle, hunt, and sacrifice marked a man as a member of the elite. On the other hand, pursuing the honor that inspired such violence entailed competition between individuals that ripped apart the aristocracy in vendettas and civil wars, and declared killing the ruler to be the apogee of fame. While one might distinguish a "good" violence in the service of rulers from other forms that were "bad," this distinction had no real reference in a world where cadet lines were also rulers who were obliged to violently serve their own territories and followers, and bellicose individuals were – in the midst of combats or hunts – the definition of a true man. The fact that "completing one's reputation" generally indicated killing or expelling one's lord precisely expresses the contradiction at the heart of a nobility defined by its violence. Without an administrative/legal system that subordinated violence to the service of a ruler, there was no way of stabilizing the world order of the Eastern Zhou. This had also been true of the Shang, where the boundaries between subjects, allies, and enemies were porous and shifting. This pattern was not unique to preimperial East Asia, but figured in the Peloponnesian War, where the agonistic contest for glory that defined the true Greek drove men to undercut their own state in pursuit of personal glory, and drove all states to pursue a war that ultimately shattered Greek power, leaving world domination to the "Great King" of Persia (and ultimately Alexander of Macedon).

The internecine wars of the Zhou nobility motivated, and in the new uses of blood covenants and legal codes provided, the mechanism for creating a new form of state.[52] Noble lineages who increased their power by recruiting the

---

[52]. Lewis, *Sanctioned Violence*, ch. 2. See also Yuri Pines, "Political, Military, and Economic Reforms: Institutional Reforms and Reformers"; Charles Sanft, "Political, Military, and Economic Reforms: Change and Continuity at the Intersection of Received History and the Material Record: Capitals, Population Registration, Oaths, and Tallies"; and Albert Galvany,

services of commoners dispersed their own control of violence, and power shifted toward those who mobilized the largest numbers of peasants to form infantry armies. The institutions that forged these armies – allocation of land in exchange for service and taxes, mutual responsibility in law and the army, military districts as the basis of civil administration, and a bureaucracy linking the peasants to the ruler – constituted the warring state. At the pinnacle of this bureaucratic–military complex, an increasingly unchallenged autocrat escaped from the old collegial authority of the nobility, who were gradually destroyed. Meanwhile, political participation was distributed among free adult males, who were all ranked on the basis of military performance. This new model of polity was most clearly theorized by the writers on statecraft, such as the authors of the *Book of Lord Shang* and the *Han Feizi*, who advocated a society structured by law-based hierarchies based on military service.

However, as noted in my book *Sanctioned Violence*, whereas the performance of ritually sanctioned violence had distinguished the aristocracy and generated their authority, in the new state the performance of violence defined those hierarchic relations that bound men in their places. As participants in military service, blood oaths, and punishments, the "common people of Warring States China obtained not authority but discipline and obedience." While slaves, convicts, and conquered peoples were the base of the new "hierarchy of being," this regime of violence performed a general "diminution of being."

The oaths sanctified through the blood of sacrifices provided the sacral foundation for the second category of regulated violence that defined the new states: the codes of law that guided the application of the rewards and punishments to control the peasants. The former were primarily titles in the hierarchy that ranked free adult males, titles that were initially rewarded for military service (as measured by the presentation of enemy heads or ears) and subsequently through paying taxes (which primarily supported the armies). The latter included beatings, mutilation, and death, with penalties mitigated by the status determined through ranks. The linking through laws of taking life with the power of language, with increasingly explicit emphasis on the latter and masking of the former, also figured in the redefinition of the sacrificial act from the feeding of potent spirits (and generation of mastery for Shang and Zhou kings through their power over human and animal victims) to the moral instruction of the participants and the virtuous potency (*de* 德) of the superior men who guided them. The moralized violence underpinning the new legal codes also

---

"Political, Military, and Economic Reforms: The Army, Wars, and Military Arts"; all in *The Oxford Handbook of Early China*, ed. Elizabeth Childs-Johnson (Oxford: Oxford University Press, 2020).

took the form of the collective liability and duty of mutual surveillance that defined the new order.

The bloody vengeance that had marked the life of the Zhou nobility – like the violence of combat, the hunt, and sacrifice – also became a moralized duty that marked one's place in the social order. Specifically, it was a debt of bloodshed that marked ties between men – both the political ties linking patron to client and the kin ties linking family members. The former derived from the model of the bravoes (*xia*) who were gathered as private armies by leading officials (often noble kin of the states' rulers) in the late Warring States. The latter was articulated in the classics and commentaries of the *ru* classicists, who used the violence of vengeance to mark the total devotion to elders and superiors that they espoused in the family and the new political order. As just sketched out, all these forms of violence that had defined the power and status of the Zhou nobility were incorporated into the Warring States polity as markers of subordinate status in both kinship and politics. Through military service, blood oaths, vengeance, and punishments, the common people of the Warring States obtained not authority but discipline and obedience.

Two important aspects of this transformation are not discussed in *Sanctioned Violence*. First, writers on statecraft and the later military treatises theorized how one could make peasants willing to die for the state by disseminating among them the ideals of honor and shame that had previously motivated the nobles to fight. This shows how thinkers of the period consciously theorized the transformation presented in *Sanctioned Violence*, and how this was central to restructuring the state through reworking the central forms of licit violence, warfare, and the associated legal ranking system. It also shows how the peasants' new participation in state violence was both an elevation of status, but also a "diminution of being" in that they were to be manipulated through rewards and punishments.

Second, there was a new use of violence to mark total devotion through self-sacrifice for a lord or patron, which contrasted with the Zhou nobles' wielding of violence to defend their own honor and that of their lineage by defeating all rivals, even the lord.[53] This eliminated the universal contest for honor that had motivated the Zhou elite and their world of constant vendetta and civil war, replacing it with a devotion that underlay the transition to a polity defined by an absolute ruler and his officials. However, it was also distinct from the world theorized by the writers on the military and on statecraft, in that it was based on the passionate commitment of individual fighters, rather than a discipline imposed by rewards and punishments. I will discuss each aspect in turn.

[53.] Lewis, *Honor and Shame in Early China*, pp. 92–95, 115–120.

Later Warring States texts theorized new values underpinning the warfare that defined the emerging polities. Theoreticians of statecraft argued that rewards and punishments would instill a sense of shame and honor in the common people, causing them to serve their ruler to the death. This invoked a diffused honor that constituted a new public realm including people who had previously been outside the political sphere. This new ideal of honor and shame based on service was also supposed to motivate officials to serve their ruler against corrupt cliques who filled the courts. However, a useful "shameless-ness" was also built into this model in the idea that cunning was essential both to rulers – who needed to constantly alter laws and norms – and officials, who had to adapt themselves to the shifting needs of their rulers.

This new sense of honor and shame is articulated in the *Book of Lord Shang*:

> Punishments suppress deviance, and rewards assist this. Shame [*xiu*], dis-grace [*ru*], toil, and suffering are what people hate; eminence [*xian*], glory [*rong*], leisure, and happiness are that for which they work. Punishments not being hated, and titles and salaries not being worth working for, prefigure the state's perishing.[54]

It also argued that anyone who suffered the humiliation of punishment could not enjoy the rewards of office, and that military service and the payment of taxes had to be the sole avenue for obtaining honor. The longing for riches and a "name," both reputation and social status, were declared to be universal human desires. If these derived only from the "single source" of the state, they became tools by which the ruler created both social order and a powerful army.[55] How peasants would die for honor or to avoid shame is also discussed in the *Han Feizi*, although it is less central in this text than using honor and shame to control officials.[56]

---

[54] *Shang Jun shu zhu yi* 商君書注譯, annotated by Gao Heng 高亨 (Beijing: Zhonghua, 1974), ch. 6, "Suan di 算地," p. 174.

[55] *Shang Jun shu*, ch. 6, "Suan di," p. 175; ch. 13, "Jin ling," pp. 276–277; ch. 18, "Hua ce," p. 389; ch. 20, "Ruo min 弱民," pp. 439–440. On the "single source" as necessary to the state's strength, see Mark Edward Lewis, *The Early Chinese Empires: Qin and Han* (Cambridge, MA: The Belknap Press of Harvard University, 2007), pp. 46–50; Yuri Pines, ed. and tr., *The Book of Lord Shang: Apologetics of State Power in Early China* (New York: Columbia University Press, 2017), pp. 17–20, 68–75, 85–87, 132–133, 172, 176, 221–222; Pines, "Social Engineering in Early China: The Ideology of the *Shangjun shu* (*Book of Lord Shang*) Revisited," *Oriens Extremus* 55 (2016), pp. 1–37. The *Han Feizi* argues that the ruler should be the "single source" of honors, which should go to soldiers, but instead are given to idlers who play at eremitism. See *Han Feizi ji shi* 韓非子集釋, annotated by Chen Qiyou 陳奇猷 (Shanghai: Renmin, 1974), ch. 17, "Gui shi," p. 940 (2).

[56] *Han Feizi ji shi*, ch. 1, "Chu jian," p. 2; ch. 4, "He Shi," p. 239; ch. 5, "Shi xie," p. 311; ch. 8, "Shou dao," pp. 491–492 (when rewards are certain, peasant warriors go to their deaths with total integrity [*si jie*]); ch. 17, "Liu fan," p. 952; ch. 18, "Ba shuo," p. 974; ch. 19, "Wu du," p. 1067; ch. 20, "Xin du," p. 1135.

Warring States military treatises also linked shame and honor to martiality. However, while these emphasized the necessity of shame among common soldiers, for the commander this emotion was dangerous. This was due to the tension between the commander's need for flexible and amoral "expedient assessment" and the constraints of a morally inspired sense of shame.[57] Thus the *Master Sun* argues:

> For the commander there are five dangers. If he insists on fighting to the death, then he can be slain. If he insists on living, then he can be taken prisoner. If he is easily angered and hasty, then he can be provoked with insults. If he insists on honor and purity [*lian jie*], then he can be disgraced. If he loves the people, then he can be worn down.[58]

Here two dangers derive from the general's sense of honor or shame, and the first is related, since fighting to the death was usually for the sake of honor. A commander who was provoked by insults or insisted on his honor and integrity could be manipulated through those feelings. As a master of cunning and manipulation, the commander in the *Master Sun* had to ignore his own honor or shame, but play upon such feelings in his opponents.

Later military texts concentrated on the troops, agreeing that a sense of shame motivated them to fight to the death. In referring to the commander, they largely linked him with the troops as someone who must be willing to die for his own honor and that of the state:

> If the people know that the ruler's loving their lives and begrudging their deaths reaches this extreme, when they encounter dangers for him, the soldiers will regard advancing to death as glorious, and life gained by retreating as disgraceful.
>
> Master Wu said, "In governing the state and regulating the army, you must instruct them with ritual, encourage them with duty, and cause them to have a sense of shame. If shame reaches a high degree then you can launch offensive campaigns, and even at a low degree you will be able to defend."
>
> To accept the mandate of command and not decline it, to destroy the enemy and only then speak of returning home, these are the proper rituals of the commander. Therefore on the day the army sets out, he thinks only of the glory that death will bring, not shamefully surviving.[59]

---

[57] Lewis, *Sanctioned Violence*, ch. 3, esp. pp. 114–133.

[58] *Sunzi zhi jie* 孫子直解, in *Ming ben wu jing qi shu zhi jie* 明本武經七書直解, ed. Liu Yin 劉寅, vol. 1 (Taipei: Shi Di Jiaoyu, 1972), ch. 8, "Jiu bian," p. 34a. See also *Liu tao zhi jie* 六韜直解, in *Ming ben wu jing qi shu zhi jie*, vol. 2, ch. 3, "Long tao," sect. 21, "Li jiang," p. 65a.

[59] *Wuzi zhi jie* 吳子, in *Ming ben wu jing qi shu zhi jie*, vol. 1, ch. 1, "Tu guo," pp. 6a, 9a; ch. 4, "Lun jiang," pp. 37a–b.

These argue that a concern for honor and a sense of shame are fundamental to both the commander and his troops, leading them to focus on the glory of dying for the state, and the disgrace of fleeing to save one's life.

Military treatises also advocated using punishments and rewards to create an obedient army:

> In warfare you consolidate the masses, examine what is beneficial, regulate any disorderly soldiers, [teach them how] to advance or stop, perfect their sense of shame, bind military laws, and inspect the punishments.
>
> Glory and profit [rewards] and shame and death [punishments], these are called the "four things to be preserved [by the ruler]."[60]

Wielding honor and shame to motivate the army also appears in the *Master Wei Liao*, one of the last Warring States military treatises:[61]

> In ancient times those who led the people placed ritual and good faith first, and only then granted titles and salaries. They put shame first, and only then punished. They put intimacy and love first, and only then controlled their bodies through law.[62]

This again insists that shame is essential to the army's conduct, linking it with punishment. However, it is distinctive in arguing that ritual, good faith, and familial love precede the state's contribution of rewards and punishments. It thus posits honor and shame as the ground from which law emerges. The priority of the social over the political is also enunciated in an argument that soldiers who retreat will be "disgraced by the masses," emphasizing their fellows' gaze as the source of discipline.[63]

The *Six Quivers*, advocated a different idea of how one got an army to fight:

> Uxorilocal sons-in-law and criminals who desired to escape their past shame can be gathered into a unit called the "Fortunate Employed" [because they were undeserving].[64]

---

[60]. *Sima fa zhi jie* 司馬法, in *Ming ben wu jing qi shu zhi jie*, vol. 1, ch. 3, "Ding jue," pp. 29a, 39b. See also ch. 1, "Tianzi zhi yi," pp. 16a–b (the ruler establishes the hierarchy of noble and base so that the people act in unison); 17a–b; p. 23b (rulers suffer defeat when they honor the violent rather than the obedient). On "bonds" as the basis of military law, see Lewis, *Sanctioned Violence*, pp. 67–78.

[61]. On dating the military treatises, see Mark Edward Lewis, "Writings on Warfare Found in Ancient Chinese Tombs," *Sino-Platonic Papers* 158 (August, 2005).

[62]. *Wei Liaozi zhi jie* 尉繚子, in *Ming ben wu jing qi shu zhi jie*, vol. 2 (Taipei: Shi Di Jiaoyu, 1972), ch. 1, sect. 4, pp. 18b–19a.

[63]. *Wei Liaozi*, ch. 4, sect. 17, p. 4a. See also ch. 3, sect. 10, p. 50a. A passage in the reconstructed version based on the Yinqueshan strips argues that troops with a true commander will heroically die for honor, while those lacking will be disgraced. See *Wei Liaozi jiao zhu* 校注, annotated by Zhong Zhaohua 鍾兆華 (Henan: Zhong Zhou Shu Hua She, 1982), p. 75, n. 8; *Wei Liaozi qian shuo* 淺說, annotated by Xu Yong 徐勇 (Beijing: Jiefang Jun Chubanshe, 1989), p. 160.

[64]. *Liu tao*, ch. 6, "Quan tao," sect. 53, "Jiao zhan," p. 48b. Uxorilocal sons-in-law, who "married" into a household to provide labor, were virtually slaves.

Here one redeemed a debased position by serving in the army. This work also cites the danger, discussed too in the *Han Feizi*, that men could take pride in personal morality rather than public service. In this case public service could be viewed as shameful, and glory gained by endangering the state:

> Fourth, when men-of-service display lofty moral integrity and resolute resistance, regarding this as heroic character, they will link up with foreign states and not honor their ruler. This harms their king's majesty. Fifth, when officials disdain titles and ranks, holding superiors in contempt, they will be ashamed to face hardship for their ruler.[65]

Thus the concern about honor and shame that had motivated violent competition among the warrior nobility was dispersed among several roles in the new state: worrying about honor or shame as a weakness in the commander's psychology, shame as an emotion instilled in the soldiers through ritual and education, concern for honor and shame as the foundation of rewards and punishments, shame as the condition of lowly people to be escaped from through army service, and the threat of those whose pride in their own virtue made them regard serving the state as disgraceful.

However, the *Stratagems of the Warring States*, a collection of model rhetorical persuasions, followed the *Zuo zhuan*'s idea that military defeat was the greatest cause for shame, and that only a victory could wipe it away. Like the *Zuo zhuan* it also denounced acknowledging the superiority of another state. Thus even while new political theories shifted emphasis from military valor to intelligence and self-sacrifice, the state's continued reliance on military success preserved the earlier values in new forms. The text also carried forward the transfer of noble values to the mass armies with the argument, which also figured in several Han texts, that defeat was a disgrace, the shame of which could be eliminated only through a subsequent victory.[66]

Another divergence in the Warring States regime of violence from the pure statist order advocated in the *Book of Lord Shang* and the *Han Feizi* was the gathering of personal retainers. For the retainers, this practice continued the private use of violence to establish one's place in the public realm. However, it shifted away from the Spring and Autumn nobility's focus on winning glory for a lineage by victory in battle, or securing personal prestige through defeating

---

[65] *Liu tao*, ch. 1, "Wen tao," sect. 9, "Shang xian," p. 26b.

[66] *Zhan guo ce*, ch. 1, "Dong Zhou," p. 5; ch. 5, "Qi san," p. 171; ch. 8, "Qi yi," p. 337; ch. 18, "Zhao yi," p. 625; ch. 19, "Zhao er," pp. 658–659; ch. 19, "Yan yi," p. 1064; ch. 27, "Han yi," pp. 930, 931; ch. 30, "Yan er," p. 1107; ch. 31, "Yan san," p. 1135. On victory wiping away the shame of defeat, see also *Huainanzi* 淮南子, ch. 13, "Fan lun," p. 222. This text makes the related argument that violent revenge cleanses the shame of an insult; see ch. 18 "Ren jian," p. 328. For this idea at the end of the Han (applied to frontier wars), see Xun Yue 荀悦, *Han ji* 漢紀 (Taiwan: Shangwu, 1971), ch. 26, pp. 262, 263.

rivals. In contrast, gathering retainers exalted heroic self-sacrifice to avenge the honor of a lord or patron, or the ethical obligation to avenge one's lord or kin. These ideals motivated the private retainers attached to leading ministers, just as bureaucrats were attached to the ruler through personal ties.[67]

The retainers' ethic of revenge and self-sacrifice expressed the total subordination built into the interpersonal ties through which the new style polity, and other associations in the period, were created.[68] It was probably transferred from the nobility to the people through the model of the "wandering bravoes" who were a major element of the free-floating population seeking service as retainers of rulers and leading ministers.[69] They were condemned by the *Han Feizi* in parallel with the "classicists," the latter being accused of disrupting the political order with their "culture/literature [*wen*]" while the former did so with their "martiality [*wu*]."[70] The status of these bravoes, and the associated retainers, depended on their total devotion to major political actors whom they served without being administrative subordinates.

The model for such devotion, celebrated for his willingness to die for recognition from his lord, was Yu Rang. Living in the early fifth century BCE, he had reportedly served two leading families in Jin state, who had not appreciated his abilities. He consequently chose to serve Zhi Bo, who "honored him to the highest degree." After Zhi Bo was slain by rival lineages, Yu Rang stated:

> A man-of-service dies for the one who appreciates him, just as a woman adorns herself for the one who pleases her. Zhi Bo appreciated me, and if I must die to avenge him, then my soul will not be ashamed.

He made several attempts to assassinate Zhi Bo's primary foe, mutilating himself to become unrecognizable. After the first attempt he was pardoned by his intended victim, who regarded him as worthy because of his devotion to Zhi Bo. When a friend suggested that he should enter the service of his victim to

---

[67]. Lewis, *Sanctioned Violence*, pp. 80–94; Yu Yingshi 余英時, *Shi yu zhongguo wenhua* 士與中國文化 (Shanghai: Shanghai Renmin, 1987), pp. 69–83.

[68]. For early imperial authors on the overwhelming status disparity between themselves and the ruler, see Yu Yingchun 于迎春, *Qin Han shi shi* 秦漢士史 (Beijing: Beijing Daxue, 2000), pp. 235–240.

[69]. Masubuchi Tatsuo 増淵龍夫. *Chūgoku kodai no shakai to kokka* 中國古代の社會と國家 (Tokyo: Kōbundō, 1962), pp. 49–136; Miyazaki Ichisada 宮崎市定, "Yūkyō ni tsuite 游俠について," in *Ajia shi kenkyū* アジア史研究 (Kyoto: Dōshōsha, 1957), vol. 1, pp. 131–50; T'ung-tsu Ch'ü, *Han Social Structure* (Seattle: University of Washington Press, 1972), pp. 161, 188–198, 232, 245–247; Lao Gan 勞榦, "Lun Handai de youxia 論漢代的游俠," in *Lao Gan xueshu lunwen ji* 勞榦學術論文集 (Taipei: Yiwen, 1976), vol. 2, pp. 1021–1036; Tao Xisheng 陶希聖, *Bianshi yu youxia* 辯士與游俠 (Shanghai: Shangwu, 1933). "Bravo" is a term for hired assassins or men of violence in late Renaissance Italy, derived from the same root as "brave."

[70]. *Han Feizi*, ch. 19, "Wu du," p. 1037.

facilitate approaching him, he explained that this would be "treasonous in serving one's lord," and his intention was to shame anyone who did this. Captured again, Yu explained why he persisted in trying to avenge Zhi Bo, while making no such effort for the other lineages that he had previously served:

> When I served the Fan and Zhonghang lineages they treated me as one of the masses, so I repaid them as such. When I came to Zhi Bo, he treated me as a true man-of-service of the state, and so I repaid him as such.

The intended victim wept in admiration for Yu Rang, acknowledging that he had completed his "fame [*ming*]" with his devotion to Zhi Bo, thus being a loyal servant who had a "sense of duty in dying for his reputation." All "men-of-service with resolve/ambition" wept on hearing of Yu Rang's death.[71]

This was a parable on honor and shame as the major motives for a man seeking a place in the early Warring States political order. Moving between lineages, he prized above all being acknowledged as a man of honor. His service depended on the recognition of his worth, the supreme value of which was marked by his resolve to die for whomever truly appreciated him. He presented himself as a model to shame those who could not meet such standards, and his fame for such actions was acknowledged by all the worthy men of his state, including his enemy. Notably, his enemy describes his self-sacrifice to serve his lord as a means of "completing his fame," which earlier would have referred to the act of killing or exiling one's lord to display heroism.

The *Han Feizi*, which advocated basing status entirely on state service, denounced the idealization of figures like Yu Rang. After praising ministers like Yi Yin or Guan Zhong, who had made their rulers kings or hegemons, it continued:

> But Yu Rang, serving as Zhi Bo's official, above was unable to clarify to him laws and techniques … and below could not guide him in controlling the masses so his state was secure. As a consequence, the chief of the Xiang clan slew Zhi Bo. Yu Rang then cut off his own nose, thus mutilating his appearance, in order to avenge Zhi Bo's death. Although this won him fame [*ming*] as someone who had mutilated himself and finally died for the sake of his master, in reality this did not bring even the slightest benefit to Zhi Bo. I regard this as contemptible, but the rulers of our time regard it as true loyalty, and honor Yu Rang.[72]

---

[71]. *Shi ji* 史記, by Sima Qian 司馬遷 (d. 86 BCE) and Sima Tan 司馬談 (165–110 BCE) (Beijing: Zhonghua, 1959), ch. 86, pp. 2519–2521. The same story, with variations in wording, appears in *Zhan guo ce*, ch. 18, "Zhao yi," pp. 597–599.

[72]. *Han Feizi*, ch. 4, "Jian jie shi chen," pp. 250–251.

The time expended in this critique shows that the norms that led to honoring Yu Rang were widespread, probably more widespread than the theories of Han Fei and his ilk.

The story of Yu Rang shows the changing links between status and violence in the Warring States. In the Spring and Autumn, improving status through violence depended on victory. Conquering increased one's honor, while losing was shameful. The shift towards winning glory through defeat hinged on choosing death, as in Yu Rang's "dying for his reputation." Yu Rang appears in a *Shi ji* chapter on assassins who, with one exception, all died as a result of their attempts. Some of them, and men who helped them, chose to die to prove loyalty to their patron. Here a chosen death in service of a superior was the ultimate seal of honor.[73] Honor based on victory had made all nobles potential rivals. Lords challenged the Zhou king, hereditary ministers the lords, and lesser nobles the hereditary ministers, because each had to surpass the others to gain honor. Glory based on the willingness to die for one's lord (or father) created a world in which the man of honor committed himself to total obedience to an unchallenged superior. Thus the emergence of the honor exemplified by Yu Rang was fundamental to the new world in which all members of the polity were subject to the ruler, and found glory in self-chosen servitude.

Links between the ethic of the bravoes and the emergent bureaucracy are exemplified in the "death for integrity or duty [*si jie* 死節 or *si yi* 死義]," which became celebrated in the late Warring States period. The *Han Feizi* used it to describe those who died for the public good, rejecting material wealth or factional interests. This included historical exemplars of dying for loyalty such as Bi Gan, officials who died in performing their duties, and peasants who willingly died in battle. These last are contrasted with scholars or hermits who were falsely honored in the period.[74] The *Springs and Autumns of Master Lü*, composed just before Qin's establishment of the empire, also celebrated dying for moral integrity.[75]

The figures who exemplified this new regime of violence exemplified by retainers were the "Four Princes": Mengchang of Qi, Pingyuan of Zhao, Chunshen of Chu, and Xinling of Wei. They were kin of their rulers and served as leading officials, often chief ministers. They extended their power by

---

[73.] *Shi ji*, ch. 86, pp. 2518, 2524, 2530, 2532–2533, 2533–2534. On death, particularly suicide, as the ultimate seal of honor and an efficacious act, see also *Shi ji*, ch. 76, p. 2357.

[74.] *Han Feizi*, ch. 6, "Jie Lao," p. 345; ch. 8, "Shou dao," p. 492 (2); ch. 18, "Liu fan," p. 948.

[75.] *Lü shi chun qiu jiao shi* 呂氏春秋校釋, ed. Chen Qiyou 陳奇猷 (Shanghai: Xuelin, 1984), ch. 9, "Zhi shi," p. 490; ch. 11, "Zhong lian," p. 587; ch. 12, "Shi jie," pp. 622–623 (2); ch. 12, "Jie li," p. 628 (2); ch. 12, "Bu qin," pp. 640, 640–641; "Xu yi," p. 648; ch. 14, "Bi ji," p. 829; ch. 19, "Li su," pp. 1233–1235; ch. 19, "Shang de," pp. 1257–1258; ch. 20, "Shi jun," pp. 1322–1323: story of Yu Rang, p. 1323; ch. 20, "Chang li," p. 1337; ch. 23, "Zhi hua," p. 1552.

attracting men of diverse skills, both civil and martial, who would loyally serve them in exchange for good treatment – including commensality – but above all for recognition as men of honor. The princes thus marked the transition from the world of the nobility to a bureaucratic state constituted by those appointed to office and bound to obedience. This was described by Jia Yi:

> These four princes were all brilliant, loyal, generous, and loving of true men. They honored worthies and esteemed men-of-service.[76]

Sima Qian devoted a chapter to each of the princes, describing how they attracted both former "retainers of feudal lords" and fugitives from justice. They provided these men with food, lodging, and sometimes salaries, thereby gathering thousands of men (conventionally "three thousand"). Prince Mengchang "treated noble or base without exception as his peers," and the other princes likewise were noted for honoring those whom they gathered. These retainers, in exchange for the recognition that they received, served their new masters, killing enemies or, in the case of Prince Mengchang, massacring a whole district that had laughed at him for being short. Sometimes they went to their deaths to justify the honor given them.[77]

The princes' rulers often grew suspicious, being told that their ministers were more famous than they were. Fearing this perversion of hierarchy, rulers drove their ministers into exile or planned to execute them.[78] Thus the Spring and Autumn era's pattern of status, in which nobles were competitors for power and honor rather than loyal servants, survived into the Warring States period and up to the establishment of the empire. At the same time, the model exemplified by Yu Rang disseminated an ideal of honor defined by loyalty, which helped transform heroic nobles into obedient officials. However, in the late Warring States there was still a competition between the states' rulers and the highest officials to attract such devoted followers.

While their numerous retainers marked the princes' status and political ambitions, the practice of attracting followers also spread throughout society. Thus Prince Xinling sought to attract a poor scholar, only to learn that the latter himself had "a retainer among the butchers in the market," whom the prince was asked to visit. Later, as often in such stories, the butcher served him as an assassin, but this shows that even a relatively poor and nonpolitical figure could develop networks of patronage. Such networks also figure in the story of Jing Ke,

---

[76.] *Shi ji*, ch. 6, p. 279.
[77.] *Shi ji*, ch. 75, 76, 77, 78. On Prince Mengchang's treatment of his retainers, and their killing of those who mocked him, see ch. 75, pp. 2353–54, 2355. On other lords honoring retainers, see ch. 76, pp. 2365, 2365–2366; ch. 77, pp. 2377, 2379, 2380, 2382–2383, 2385; ch. 78, p. 2395 (2).
[78.] *Shi ji*, ch. 75, pp. 2357, 2358, 2361; ch. 77, pp. 2377–2378, 2382, 2384; ch. 78, p. 2395.

who tried to assassinate the First Emperor.[79] Thus, creating networks through bestowing honor had become a general practice in Warring States society, of which the political uses, including forming bureaucracies, were an extension.

The *Shi ji* also narrates how the number of retainers dissuaded other states from attacking, or how retainers acted as private armies:

> I once passed through Xue [Prince Mengchang's city], and the customs of the youths in its neighborhoods tended to be violent, bloodthirsty, and heroic; they were completely different from those of Zou and Lu [old homes of Confucius and Mencius]. I asked why, and they said, "Prince Mengchang attracted those in the world who acted as bravoes, more than 60,000 villains with their families." The world transmits that Prince Mengchang was pleased with himself for his love of retainers, and this reputation was indeed not empty.[80]

This anecdote, part of a pattern in which Sima Qian attributes the character of regions to the impact of earlier eminences, is remarkable only in the number of those attracted. That such numerous retainers threatened public order is indicated in the account of how King Zheng, later First Emperor, asserted personal power against his mother by executing her lover, Lao Ai. He also stripped Lao Ai's 4,000 retainers of their ranks, confiscated their wealth, and exiled them to Sichuan. While he had also planned to demote the chief minister, Lü Buwei, he hesitated to act because of the large numbers of retainers and private followers who circulated through the states on his behalf. Finally, the number of private retainers from other rulers who visited Lü Buwei led the king to demand his exile, and ultimately his suicide.[81]

This worry in Qin about private retainers whose loyalty to their patrons surpassed that to the state also figures in the legal materials excavated at Shuihudi:

> When a mission is sent to a foreign state or an outer vassal state, and a state subject or an assistant clerk of the emissary does not return, [the emissary] is not implicated. What is meant by "state subject" and "assistant clerk"? This means followers or clerks who were not private retainers of the emissary.[82]

[79.] *Shi ji*, ch. 77, p. 2378; ch. 86, pp. 2528, 2530, 2534.

[80.] *Shi ji*, ch. 76, pp. 2366, 2369; ch. 77, pp. 2377, 2379–2380. For the passage quoted, see ch. 75, p. 2363. On Sima Qian's explaining customs through the lingering influence of historical figures, see Lewis, *The Construction of Space in Early China* (Albany: SUNY Press, 2006), pp. 210–211. On youths as prone to wildness and linked to *xia*, see *Construction of Space*, pp. 163–168, 187–188.

[81.] *Shi ji*, ch. 6, p. 227; ch. 85, pp. 2512–2513.

[82.] *Shuihudi Qin mu zhujian* 睡虎地秦墓竹簡 (Beijing: Wenwu, 1978), pp. 227–228, D159; A. F. P. Hulsewé, *Remnants of Ch'in Law: An Annotated Translation of the Ch'in Legal and Administrative Rules of the 3rd Century B.C. Discovered in Yün-meng Prefecture, Hu-pei Province, in 1975* (Leiden: E. J. Brill, 1985), pp. 172–173. The preceding text refers to restrictions imposed on "retainers of the ruler of a foreign state" coming as emissaries. See *Shuihudi Qin mu zhujian*, pp. 227–228, D158.

Elements in Ancient East Asia

This distinguishes the state's subjects from the private retainers of an official, and it makes the official liable for the latter, just as he would be liable for the crimes of kin. A fragment of a statute discovered in the same tomb imposes a fine on any prefecture where "wandering men-of-service" are found without proper credentials, and this is linked to members of the Qin population who have departed the state.[83] This shows Qin's desire to control the movement of its population, its worries about the travel of other states' private retainers, and its fear of private retainers attached to its own officials. It also indicates that such retainers were legally recognized at least into the era of imperial Qin.

One last aspect of the Warring States transformation of violence was the incorporation of the supreme autocrat – who marked the culmination of the hierarchies and total devotion discussed earlier – into the understanding of war, as expressed in the doctrine of *yi bing* 義兵 (roughly like the Western idea of "just war").[84] This justified war as a mode of punishment carried out by the highest authority to create social order, making all proper combat a manifestation of the power of the chief lawgiver and highest judge. It was first sketched in Warring States philosophical texts, like the *Xunzi*, and culminated in Qin in the *Springs and Autumns of Master Lü* and the First Emperor's stone inscriptions. It was carried forward into the Han in the *Huainanzi* and *Shi ji*, in the debates on the salt and iron monopolies where it justified an activist emperor, and in the Eastern Han, as in the chapter on punishments in the *Han shu*, which presented itself as a history of warfare, as well as other texts.[85]

Before discussing violence under the early empires, it is useful to contrast Warring States developments with the late Roman Republic, where armies based on universal, citizen obligations were replaced in the long first century BCE by professional armies whose primary loyalty was to their commander. This began with reforms under Marius in 107 BCE that "proletarianized" the

---

[83] *Shuihudi Qin mu zhujian*, pp. 129–130, C3; Hulsewé, *Remnants of Ch'in Law*, p. 104.

[84] Mark Edward Lewis, "The Just War in Early China," in *The Ethics of War in Asian Civilizations: A Comparative Perspective*, ed. Torkel Brekke (London: Routledge, 2006), pp. 185–200.

[85] See, for example, Wang Fu 王符 (ca. 82–167 CE), *Qian fu lun jian* 潛夫論箋, annotated by Wang Jipei 汪繼培 (Beijing: Zhonghua, 1979), ch. 5, sect. 23, "Bian yi," p. 272:

"Armies intimidate the deviant and illuminate civilizing virtue. Thus the sage rises and rebels are eliminated. Lord Huan of Qi, Lord Wen of Jin, and Lord Xiang of Song were regional lords in an age of decline, but they were still ashamed that states were destroyed, and they could not save them. How much more should a world ruler who has the mandate from august Heaven? The hereditary officials of Jin and Chu were officials of lesser states, but were still ashamed that anyone should infringe on their persons. How much more should the highest officials and those employed by the Son of Heaven? ... A single person sighing damages the royal Way, how much more the slaughter of tens of thousands?"

Here, war maintains social order and prevents people's suffering. While acknowledging the limited virtue of Spring and Autumn nobles who used warfare to save states or to defend their own honor, the author argues that such conduct was inferior to that of the new rulers.

army by opening it to all citizens. In subsequent decades, poorer soldiers came to rely on pay, on portions of booty, and ultimately on rewards of land upon retirement. In this period the republican empire was created by ambitious political figures (beginning with Marius and Sulla and continuing through the Triumvirates up to Octavian), who gained command of armies, conquered other states, rewarded their men with the booty, and elevated their own position through the loyalty of their forces. This culminated in the establishment of the empire/principate by Augustus and his successors, whose political power was based on their control of the now completely professional armies.[86] This contrast between an imperial state based on the ruler's unique relation with a professional army and the Chinese case of a state built on universal peasant service marks one of the clearest differences between the roughly contemporary Principate and Antonine rulers in Rome, and the early empires in East Asia.

Violence under the Early Empires

The Qin conquest of all the other states brought an end to the Warring States period and created the unitary empire as a political form in East Asia, marked by a new regime of violence. This is clearly articulated in the stele inscriptions of the First Emperor, which are our most important evidence for the self-representation of imperial Qin.[87] These inscriptions celebrate the achievements of the First Emperor, and the shifting use of violence figures prominently. They depict warfare as existing from earliest times down to the immediate past, describing it as chaos and criminality, with cruel rulers launching savage wars to extend their power. The First Emperor, in contrast, launched "punitive attacks against the rebellious and recalcitrant [*tao fa luan ni* 討伐亂逆]," thereby ending wars and bestowing peace upon the world. He wielded "martial order/ rightness [*wu yi* 武義]" to straighten out the world, and tore down all interstate walls or difficult landscape that blocked communication. His use of violence against rival states is described as punishing or executing (*zhu* 誅) them, thus

---

[86]. The clearest account is Antonio Santosuosso, *Storming the Heavens: Soldiers, Emperors, and Civilians in the Roman Empire* (Boulder, CO: Westview, 2004), ch. 1–2, 5–6. See also Greg Woolf, *Rome: An Empire's Story* (Oxford: Oxford University Press, 2012), ch. 1–12, esp. ch. 9, 11; Mary Beard, *SPQR: A History of Ancient Rome* (New York: W. W. Norton, 2015), ch. 6, 7, 9; David Potter, *The Origin of Empire: Rome from the Republic to Hadrian* (Cambridge, MA: Harvard University Press, 2019), ch. 17–25; Lendon, *Soldiers and Ghosts*, ch. 10–11.

[87]. On the inscriptions, their political and cultural background, and their uses as evidence, see Martin Kern, *The Stele Inscriptions of Ch'in Shih-huang: Text and Ritual in Early Chinese Imperial Representation* (New Haven: American Oriental Society, 2000). On their role within a program of Qin self-representation and communication with its people, see Charles Sanft, *Communication and Cooperation in Early Imperial China: Publicizing the Qin Dynasty* (Albany: SUNY Press, 2014).

absorbing the violence of warfare into its use in law. This is significant, because passages describe his establishment of laws and credit these with ending wars, and correcting all deviant customs.[88]

The First Emperor here presented himself as having achieved a revolutionary rupture with earlier history.[89] However, writing in the early Han, Jia Yi argued that Qin's rapid fall was due to its failure to break with its *own* past. Despite having united the world to end any need for warfare, it sought to rule through the same methods by which it had conquered its rivals, specifically "exalting deceit and force [*gao zha li* 高詐力]" – that is, warfare. Having structured itself on enlisting peasants for military service, and ranking them thereby, Qin's proclaimed ending of warfare took the form of mobilization for offensives against regions beyond the frontier, the building of walls in the north, and the construction of roads to facilitate the movement of officials and armies. A state created for warfare and expansion, it wasted its resources – and alienated newly conquered people – by fighting when there were no useful worlds to conquer, and launching building projects that served no purpose except war (or the eternal commemoration in its capital of past victories).[90]

This again merits contrast with Rome. As discussed earlier, the founder of the Roman principate, Augustus, inherited the pattern of deriving political power from his command of a professional army. In contrast with the problem presented by universal military service to Qin and, as will be discussed later, the Western Han, the Roman military system was well suited to serving in a world empire. From the beginning the army created the emperor, although as Tacitus argues this only became obvious in the year of the four emperors (69 CE), when these rulers were each enthroned by their own armies.

The Western Han adopted most of its institutions from Qin, which was its only model of a universal empire. As for the regime of violence, the most important fields were the military and the law, which will be sequentially discussed. While they no longer needed to mobilize mass infantry armies to fight hostile neighbors, the Western Han adopted Qin's universal military

---

[88]. On the universality of war and the savagery of earlier rulers, see Kern, *Stele Inscriptions*, pp. 12, 13, 36, 38–39, 46. On the First Emperor's punitive attacks or punishments, see pp. 12, 31 (*zhu*), 38, 41–42 (*zhu*). On ending wars, see pp. 14, 21, 32, 39. On eliminating walls and obstructive topography, see pp. 42–43. On establishing laws and punishments, see pp. 17, 26, 29, 32, 35, 37, 38–39 (here his sage laws extinguished all rival states, and "forever halted clashes of arms"), 47–48. On the Warring States critique of custom, Qin's invocation of this idea to justify its use of laws and punishments, and the Han application of the same criticism to Qin, see Lewis, *Construction of Space*, pp. 192–212.

[89]. Yuri Pines, "The Messianic Emperor: A New Look at Qin's Place in China's History," in *Birth of an Empire: The State of Qin Revisited*, ed. Yuri Pines, Lothar von Falkenhausen, Gideon Shelach, and Robin D. S. Yates (Berkeley: University of California Press, 2014), ch. 8.

[90]. *Shi ji*, ch. 6, pp. 280–281, 283; Lewis, *Early Chinese Empires*, pp. 70–74.

service and related ranking of the population. However, as Jia Yi's critique of Qin pointed out, such an institution was both wasteful and dangerous for a world empire where combat was primarily waged at distant frontiers against mounted, nomadic foes. Fighting against the Xiongnu, the Han made incremental changes that led to the creation of a new style of army, one which had radical consequences for the subsequent history of empires in East Asia.[91]

The ineffectiveness of Han infantry armies against the Xiongnu cavalry was demonstrated by the defeat of Gaozu's army at Baideng in 200 BCE. Under Emperor Wen, they began to breed horses for battle and, in 178 BCE, to train cavalry.[92] This continued on a larger scale when Emperor Wu launched his wars against the Xiongnu in 133 BCE. The infantry armies lost any utility after the suppression of the royal domains in 154 BCE, which ended the prospect of internal warfare. Besides expertise in cavalry, armies fighting the Xiongnu needed men skilled with the crossbow. Both of these required protracted training that could not be acquired in the annual training sessions of peasant levies. Consequently, Emperor Wu and his successors increasingly had peasants pay a tax in lieu of service, and used the income to hire long-term recruits.

After the civil war that in 23 CE ended Wang Mang's attempt to establish a new dynasty, a combination of penury, recognition that peasant levies were primarily loyal to local powers (as they had shown in the civil war), and the knowledge that such levies were useless in the frontier wars that were the state's primary need led in 32 CE to the abolition of the annual fall training and the elimination of the local military official (*du wei* 都尉). This meant that peasant soldiers became strictly emergency levies used to respond to bandits, and that universal service ceased to be the organizing principle of the state. Instead, the Eastern Han relied on surrendered nomads who were resettled inside the frontiers under their chieftains, professional military commands of long-term recruits in the capital and at the frontier, and pardoned convicts who refilled the ranks of these recruits. In the short term, this relieved Han peasants from the burden of annual service, and it allowed the formation of large-scale cavalry armies that were able to defeat the Xiongnu in the late first century CE. This new army also allowed for a relative demilitarization of the interior.

These innovations set the pattern for armies in subsequent East Asian dynasties. Mass levies, which were militarily inferior and politically dangerous, did not reappear as a regular institution until the end of the imperial system in the twentieth century. Instead, variations of the Eastern Han policies of "using

---

[91.] This largely follows Mark Edward Lewis, "The Han Abolition of Universal Military Service," in *Warfare in Chinese History*, ed. Hans J. van de Ven (Leiden: E. J. Brill, 2000), pp. 33–75.

[92.] Nicola Di Cosmo, *Ancient China and its Enemies* (Cambridge: Cambridge University Press, 2004), pp. 196, 199, 203–204, 231, 233.

barbarians to control barbarians," using convicts as a source of manpower, demilitarizing the interior, and forming professional armies at the frontier became standard – in diverse scales and forms – through subsequent empires. Mass levies appeared only as an emergency procedure. Powerful local families also anticipated another source of soldiery – hereditary military households – as they militarized their local bases in response to disorder in the late Eastern Han. Whereas in the late Warring States, Qin, and Western Han military obligation and associated ranks had defined the social order, in the Eastern Han participating in combat was restricted to people who were marginal to conventional society: nomads (sometimes become partially sedentary), convicts, and professional military men whose lives and status blurred with the preceding two categories.

The ultimate failure of the Eastern Han armies, and fall of the dynasty, also prefigured later imperial states. Once the Xiongnu had been defeated, bonuses for taking heads that had rewarded surrendered nomads disappeared, and as they were still loyal to their own chiefs, they increasingly became a threat inside the Han frontier. Similarly, these forces, and northern fortifications, did not protect against the rebellions in the second century CE of Qiang tribesmen who had been resettled inside the western frontier. Without standing forces, administrators from the east routinely fled, and western commanderies were often abandoned. The professional armies increasingly became the creatures of their commanders, who unlike in Western Han practice remained at their posts for years and even decades. As social order in the interior decayed, provincial governors – who had earlier been inspectors – became autonomous actors commanding private armies. Locally powerful families, forced to provide their own security, also developed private forces that together with neighbors, or politically ambitious warlords, formed substantial armies. At the end of the Eastern Han these diverse private forces all figured in the wars against religious rebels and the fight to control the capital that triggered the fall of the dynasty.

This history of imperial collapse due to resettled "barbarians" entering the service of rival commanders or rulers, and of armies becoming the private tools of their generals, resembles that of Rome. As argued by Michael Kulikowski, during the fourth century CE competing emperors waged murderous civil wars, each commanding private armies and recruiting barbarian tribesmen. In the fifth century this became a more general warlordism, where larger numbers of officers fought for smaller geographic stakes, again with barbarians supporting rival Roman contenders. This mutual slaughter undertaken by Roman rulers and commanders finally brought an end to Roman rule in the west (while Byzantium continued to wax and wane in the eastern Mediterranean for a millennium). Other scholars have also argued that the central political problem in the Roman west was at the level of emperors and generals. The "barbarian invaders" were largely supporting other men's interests until the very end.[93]

In addition to warfare, the most important use of violence in the early East Asian empires was in legal punishments. Apart from other aspects of law – general principles, codes and legal language, judicial authorities and procedures, relation to the social order and religion, role as a source of labor – punishments have remained a central topic.[94] Indeed, the first account of law in East Asia – chapter 23 of Ban Gu's *Han shu*, entitled "Treatise on the Norms of Punishment [*xing fa zhi* 刑法志]" – deals entirely with the uses of violence in a narrow sense, beginning with an account of the history of warfare and then discussing the evolving forms of mutilating punishments. Thus while the law performed many functions, it was often understood as a form of applied violence.

As for the multitude of functions, Barbieri-Low and Yates have argued that law in the early empires provided "idealized blueprints for the construction of the engine of the state and the instruction manual for the officials to operate."[95] They then list and discuss the major functions of these laws: (1) controlling public order; (2) establishing rules for legal procedures; (3) managing state finances and the state's fundamental economic activities; (4) managing and controlling the bureaucracy; (5) managing the flow of information, communications, and personnel; (6) controlling ideology and religious practices; (7) managing and exploiting the labor power of the population; (8) projecting

---

[93.] Michael Kulikowski, *The Tragedy of Empire: From Constantine to the Destruction of Roman Italy* (Cambridge, MA: Belknap Press of Harvard University, 2019); Santosuosso, *Storming the Heavens*, ch. 8; Peter Heather, *The Fall of the Roman Empire: A New History of Rome and the Barbarians* (Oxford: Oxford University Press, 2005), ch. 2, 4, 10; Walter Goffart, *Barbarians and Romans, A.D. 418–584* (Princeton: Princeton University Press, 1980); Goffart, *Barbarian Tides: The Migration Age and the Later Roman Empire* (Philadelphia: University of Pennsylvania Press, 2006); Adrian Goldsworthy, *The Fall of the West: The Death of the Roman Superpower* (London: Weidenfield and Nicolson, 2009), Parts 2–3, Conclusion; Chris Wickham, *The Inheritance of Rome: Illuminating the Dark Ages, 400–1000* (New York: Penguin, 2009), ch. 4.

[94.] Anthony J. Barbieri-Low and Robin D. S. Yates, *Law, State, and Society in Early Imperial China: A Study with Critical Edition and Translation of the Legal Texts from Zhangjjiashan Tomb no. 247, vol. 1–2* (Leiden: E. J. Brill, 2015); A. F. P Hulsewé, *Remnants of Han Law, vol. 1: Introductory Studies and Annotated Translation of Chapters 22 and 23 of the History of the Former Han Dynasty* (Leiden: E. J. Brill, 1955); *Remnants of Ch'in Law*; "Ch'in and Han Law," in *The Cambridge History of China, vol. 1: The Ch'in and Han Empires*, ed. Denis Twitchett and Michael Loewe (Cambridge: Cambridge University Press, 1986), pp. 520–544; Ulrich Lau and Thies Staack, *Legal Practice in the Formative Stages of the Chinese Empire: An Annotated Translation of the Exemplary Qin Criminal Cases from the Yuelu Academy Collection* (Leiden: E. J. Brill, 2016); Lewis, *Early Chinese Empires*, ch. 10.

[95.] Barbieri-Low and Yates, *Law, State, and Society in Early Imperial China*, vol. 1, p. 210. On law's major functions, see pp. 210–219. See also Lewis, *Early Chinese Empires*, pp. 232–237, for a discussion of how law modeled the entire social structure in the patterns of punishments and collective responsibility.

state power into the heart of each family; (9) monopolizing and organizing the status system (i.e., the system of ranks); (10) managing the army. Thus the laws regulated criminal matters, much administration, the control of officials, religious and intellectual practices (e.g., regulations on sacrifice, and control of writings), extraction of labor to build the state's infrastructure, the form of families, and the status rankings of the population. These ranks, in turn, shaped the application of punishments, as they could be surrendered in lieu of suffering mutilation or fines.

While the secondary literature examines the evolving categories and forms of punishments, legal texts as a special form of language, the specialized legal experts who were the masters of that language, and the patterns of legal enquiries and trials, here I will discuss how different social categories were subjected to different forms of legal violence, which marked their distinctive relations with the ruler. This includes four categories: (1) commoners, (2) officials, (3) powerful local families, and (4) eunuchs. The last three categories were distinguished not in formal rules prescribed in the legal codes, but in practices that became conventional. In this they paralleled, as will be discussed, the status of revenge as a form of violence that became normative without being legal.

Commoners were the primary targets of laws dealing with crimes, administration, and labor. They received ranks as gifts from the emperor, initially largely for military service and paying money to the army. Ranks were also given to mark auspicious occasions such as the birth of an imperial offspring or naming of an heir, and even with the celebration of some annual holiday, so that they began to roughly parallel age. In the event of violating a law people could remit their ranks, but also pay fines, or even suffer mutilation. As Ban Gu discusses in his monograph, mutilations were replaced by Emperor Wen with beatings with a bastinado as a form of mercy that avoided permanent disfigurement. However, the strokes were so numerous that people usually died, and when the number was reduced to avert this, punishments began to lose their deterrent effect. For major crimes, punishment could also entail mutual implication of kin (or military squads) so that the range of punishments mapped out the social groupings that the state held to be significant. Finally, laws controlled routine labor service, and many legal punishments entailed additional work.

While officials and Liu family kings were in theory also subject to this system, certain thinkers argued for the need to distinguish them through a differential pattern of violence. Jia Yi (200–168 BCE) wrote several essays on how the ruler's and ministers' statuses were linked, and how not shaming them was crucial. Most important was "Steps and Degrees," which begins with a metaphor linking the statuses of ruler and ministers:

The exalted honor of the ruler is like a great hall, the collective ministers like the steps, and the masses like the ground. Thus if there are nine steps upward, then the floor of the hall [*lian* 廉, also "honor"] is far from the ground, and the hall is lofty. If there were no steps, then the floor would be close to the ground, and the hall would be lowly. What is lofty is hard to clamber up, but what is lowly is easy to ascend/humiliate ... So the ancient sage kings constructed steps or degrees; on the inside hereditary ministers, on the outside the regional nobility, and only then the officials and minor clerks, reaching down to the commoners. These steps and degrees being clear, the Son of Heaven was placed on top. Therefore his honor was unreachable.

A village saying says, "In throwing something at a rat, avoid the vessels." ... If the rat is near the vessels, then you will be afraid and not throw at it, because you fear harming the vessels. How much closer are the noble ministers to the ruler! So he uses honor, shame, and regulated rituals to control the noble men, granting them death [i.e., permitting suicide] without the disgrace of public execution. According to ritual, one does not inspect the teeth of the ruler's horses, and stepping on their fodder would merit punishment. You must rise on seeing even the armrest and staff of the ruler, get down from your horse on encountering his carriage, scurry [as a sign of respect] on entering the main hall, and no disgraceful punishment is applied to his favorite ministers. This is all to honor the ruler. These are how you remove the ruler from any possibility of disrespect, and by which you make the great ministers honorable and heighten their integrity [*jie*].

From the regional kings and the highest ministers, all are people for whom the Son of Heaven adopts a respectful appearance and treats them with full ritual ... If you cause them to be subjected to the same laws as the masses – to be tattooed, have their noses cut off, heads shaved, legs cut off, be whipped, cursed, executed, and exposed in the market – then wouldn't the hall have no steps? Wouldn't the disgrace of public execution impinge too closely on the ruler? If the sense of honor and shame is not practiced, then wouldn't the great ministers be unable to wield important powers, and wouldn't the high officers have shameless heart/minds like the lowest menials?[96]

This elaborates the need to distinguish officials and regional kings from ordinary people by not subjecting the former to mutilating punishments. It also links this to the classicist model that punishments should not be applied to noble men, nor ritual to commoners.[97]

---

[96] *Han shu* 漢書, by Ban Gu et al. (Beijing: Zhonghua, 1962), ch. 48, pp. 2254–2255. For another version, see *Jiazi xin shu jiaoshi* 賈子新書校釋, annotated by Qi Yuzhang 祁玉章 (Taipei: Qi Yuzhang, 1974), ch. 2, "Jie ji," pp. 241–282; ch. 7, "Lun cheng," p. 867.

[97] *Li ji zhu shu* 禮記注疏 in *Shisan jing zhushu*, vol. 5 (Taipei: Yiwen, 1974), ch. 3, "Qu li shang," p. 6a; *Han shu*, ch. 48, p. 2257 (quoting Jia Yi): "Therefore in ancient times ritual did not reach the common people, and punishments did not reach the hereditary officials." See also the late Eastern Han *Extended Reflections;* Xun Yue, *Shen jian* 申鑒, *in Xin bian zhuzi ji cheng*, vol. 2 (Taipei: Shijie, 1974), ch. 1, "Zheng ti," pp. 2–3: "Ritual and the teachings of glory and disgrace are applied to the noble man to transform his emotions. Fetters, handcuffs, whips, and cudgels are applied to the petty person to control him"; *Kongzi jia yu* 孔子家語, annotated by Wang Su

This is also significant for arguing that the Son of Heaven's honor depended on honoring his officials, implying likewise that the honor of the officials depended upon that of the ruler. Thus, the honor of the entire government rose and fell together. While the officials' sentiments were inspired by the ruler, they had to be absorbed by the officials, who thus developed a sense of shame, regulated themselves with ritual, and became willing to kill themselves for the state.

Jia Yi also insisted that their being controlled by honor and shame, and thus being self-regulating, contrasted with the pursuit of profit that characterized ordinary people:

> If the ruler treats his great ministers like he treats his dogs and horses, they will conduct themselves like dogs and horses. If he treats them like the mass of ordinary officials, they will conduct themselves as ordinary officials. Stupid, vulgar, and shameless; unprincipled and unconstrained; honor and shame will not be established, and they will have no self-esteem. They will indiscriminately approve of anything, going after any profit they see and snatching any convenience ...
>
> [Ideally] if they commit a major crime, then accepting his orders they will face north, bow twice, kneel, and cut their own throats. He will not have them seized and punished, but will say, "High officials will sometimes commit errors, but I treat them with ritual." Because he treats them with ritual, the officials will delight in themselves, be constrained by honor and shame, and devote themselves to good conduct ... Focusing on good conduct and forgetting profit, they will hold to the regulations and rely on duty. So the ruler can let them wield uncontrolled power, and entrust to them an infant heir.[98]

Other Han authors argued that concern for profit produced a mind that could not focus on the public good, and so was inappropriate for officials. Thus the difference in officials' place in the hierarchy of violence was an extension of their distinctive psychology.[99]

Han legal practice adopted these ideas. When high officials committed crimes, they were often granted the privilege of committing suicide rather than suffering mutilating punishments and the exposure of their corpses in the marketplace. The best-known example is Sima Qian, who was sentenced to

---

王肅 (CE 195–256), in *Xin bian zhu zi jicheng*, vol. 2, ch. 3, p. 29; ch. 7, p. 71. On these arguments, see Charles Sanft, "Rituals that Don't Reach, Punishments that Don't Impugn: Jia Yi on the Exclusions From Punishment and Ritual," *Journal of the American Oriental Society* 125.1 (2005), pp. 31–44.

[98.] *Han shu*, ch. 48, pp. 2256–2258.

[99.] Lu Jia 陸賈, *Xin yu jiao zhu* 新語校注 (Beijing: Zhonghua, 1986), ch. 1, "Dao ji," p. 53; ch. 6, "Shen wei," p. 91; ch. 9, "Huai lü," p. 129; *Huainanzi*, ch. 13, "Fan lun," p. 215; *Kongzi jia yu*, ch. 12, "Dizi xing," p. 28.

death, had this commuted to castration, and was expected to commit suicide. He chose not to do so in order to complete his great history, but the fact remains that as an official he was not subjected to the full rigors of the law. Although such "mercy" towards officials was not invariable, not subjecting them to public punishment became conventional.

A second category in the Han distinguished by the differential application of legal violence, in this case its extraordinary severity, comprised the powerful local families in the Western Han, particularly under Emperor Wu. Such families had been targeted since the beginning of the dynasty for resettlement in cities erected at imperial mausolea north of Chang'an, and by legal restrictions on landholdings. Emperor Wu, in order to raise money for wars against the Xiongnu and suppress local threats, employed legal specialists to use the law to destroy such families and confiscate their wealth. These men, described in the chapter on "cruel clerks [*ku li* 酷吏]" in the *Shi ji*, manipulated the letter of the law to secure the desired results, and through their ability to thus gratify the emperor's desires they often rose to dominate the court.

Thus Zhang Tang 張湯 came up with laws to curtail powerful bureaucrats, regional lords, and powerful families, often managing to eliminate the last and to confiscate their wealth. He would refer to the emperor to deliberate a verdict for difficult cases, and the emperor's verdict would be recorded and used as a precedent.[100] He eventually rose to become Palace Counsellor and his influence at court overshadowed that of the Chancellor. Other officials described in less detail who also rose to dominate the court through using the law to destroy local powers included Yi Zong 益縱 and Wang Wenshu 王溫舒.[101] Sima Qian accuses these men of manipulating the legal system on their own behalf, but they also showed how the law could be specially applied to overly powerful elements of the population in order to strengthen the emperor's position.

A last category drawn into a distinctive relation to the emperor through legal violence was the eunuchs. As most dramatically demonstrated in the case of Sima Qian, those castrated for some crime could become close personal attendants of the emperor, were fawned on by high officials who sought to curry their favor, and in certain periods came to dominate the empire. Several texts state that people, including officials, might even seek to be castrated in order to gain influence as eunuchs.[102] While not all eunuchs had been reduced

---

[100.] Sima Qian, *Shi ji*, ch. 122, pp. 3136–3138, 3139, 3140.

[101.] Sima Qian, *Shi ji*, ch. 122, pp. 3146, 3147–3150.

[102.] *Han Feizi*, ch. 17, "Gui shi," p. 940 (officials feel no shame in being disgraced through castration to become eunuchs); Huan Kuan 桓寬, *Yan tie lun* 鹽鐵論, In *Xin bian zhuzi jicheng*, vol. 2, #57, "Zhou Qin," p. 59.

to that status through punishment, the category nevertheless provides another form of those who through legal violence achieved a distinctive relationship with the emperor.

The categories just listed show how the emperor could wield legal power through imposing forms of violence outside conventional channels, but he was also the most important figure *within* the legal system. As the supreme lawgiver, he decided all legal cases involving nobles and high officials, and he could protect them or punish them according to his wishes. These cases had to be referred to the emperor for final sentencing because only he possessed the authority to punish these privileged groups. As pointed out by Hulsewé, the rule to seek the emperor's consent regarding punishing nobles and high minis-ters was established by the Han founder in 200 BCE, and continued in effect until the end of the Western Han. Such permission had to be granted before officials of a salary of 600 piculs or more could be punished.[103]

The emperor thus stood at the apogee of the law, or in practice above it, using it as a tool to control the nobility, powerful families, and officials at court. A discussion between Du Zhou and a retainer summarizes this:

> The way [Du Zhou] dealt with political matters imitated that of Zhang Tang, and he was skilled in divining the emperor's wishes. Whoever the emperor wished to eliminate, he would entrap. Whoever the emperor wished to pardon, [Du] would keep him imprisoned awaiting further instructions, while making it seem that he had been unjustly accused. One of his retainers criticized him saying, "You are responsible for assisting the Son of Heaven to justly deliberate on cases but ignore the statutes, instead deciding cases according to the emperor's wishes. Is that what a legal official should do?" Zhou replied: "How were the statutes created? What was regarded as just by earlier rulers was compiled into statutes, and what was regarded as just by later rulers was recorded as ordinances. What suits the times is right, so why bother with laws of former times?"[104]

Thus people who dominated the court recognized the power of the emperor as supreme lawgiver, accepting earlier laws as the desires of earlier rulers, and creating ordinances to further the current ruler's political agenda.

While Sima Qian disapproved, this indicates actual practice. Legal docu-ments discovered in recent decades show that the emperor could create new laws or change existing ones through drafting ordinances in response to specific cases. As noted by Barbieri-Low and Yates, these ordinances "could also be used to create new institutions or make major revisions to state policy," and their legal status came directly from the verbal authority of the emperor.[105] The

---

[103.] Hulsewé, *Remnants of Han Law*, pp. 285–296.   [104.] Sima Qian, *Shi ji*, ch. 122, p. 3153.
[105.] Barbieri-Low and Yates, *Law, State, and Society in Early Imperial China*, sect. 3.28, p. 1112.

Ordinances on Fords and Passes found at Zhangjiashan shows how such ordinances came into effect. The emperor could instruct the Chancellor or Chief Prosecutor to draft legislation to address a particular problem, and they would draft a petition. Alternatively, they could petition the emperor directly with a proposed ordinance drafted by themselves or by another high official. In both cases, the ordinances were put into effect simply with verbal approval from the emperor: "It should be done [ke 可]." In some cases, the proposed ordinance would be discussed in a court deliberation before the Chief Prosecutor forwarded it to the emperor for the final decision.[106]

Another demonstration of the emperor's legal power was his right to pardon all but the most serious crimes. As Brian McKnight showed in his study of both amnesties and great acts of grace (distinguished by the range of those pardoned), the practice of pardons seems to have begun at the beginning of the empire, and it was used with great frequency throughout the Han and into later dynasties (but never as frequently as in the Han).[107] Whatever the motives for these amnesties, routinely given in response to some happy event for the imperial house or to quell prodigies, they served to display the emperor's life-giving virtue and his concern for the people's well-being. These regular pardons also became fundamental to the extralegal endorsement of vengeance in the Han, where avengers often benefited from great acts of grace.

They also displayed the fact that the emperor was the source of law, since this underlay his power to suspend its regular practice. Here, one could cite the idea – formulated by Carl Schmitt and developed by Giorgio Agamben and Paul Kahn – of the "state of exception," in which sovereign power is defined by the right to suspend the routine functioning of law.[108] This ability to unmake laws also manifests itself in more routine practices such as – in Western thought –

[106.] Barbieri-Low and Yates, *Law, State, and Society in Early Imperial China*, pp. 1112–1113. For the complete account of the law, its significance, and its formulation, see pp. 1112–1145. The process could require an additional step if it emerged from court deliberation. Thus in ordinance no. 12, the Chancellor of State put forward an ordinance regarding the purchase of horses, owned by private individuals or the state, by Commandery Governors. Following deliberation by the court, the petition was forwarded to the Chief Prosecutor who petitioned the emperor and made some additions to the proposal. Finally, the two petitions were combined into one and submitted to the emperor for verbal approval. See p. 1117.

[107.] Brian E. McKnight, *The Quality of Mercy: Amnesties and Traditional Chinese Justice* (Honolulu: University of Hawai'i Press, 1981), esp. ch. 2, "The Early Empire."

[108.] Carl Schmitt, *Political Theology: Four Chapters on the Concept of Sovereignty*, tr. George Schwab (Chicago: University of Chicago Press, 1985 [1922, rev. ed. 1934]); Giorgio Agamben, *State of Exception*, tr. Kevin Attell (Chicago: University of Chicago Press, 2005) (pp. 11–22 present ideas on the state of exception in Western states, and historical cases of their use); Paul W. Kahn, *Political Theology: Four New Chapters on the Concept of Sovereignty* (New York: Columbia University Press, 2011); John P. McCormick, "The Dilemmas of Dictatorship: Carl Schmitt and Constitutional Emergency Powers," in *Law as Politics: Carl*

pardons, the treatment of pirates as the "enemy of all mankind" who lay beyond legal protection, and "jury nullification," which in English law since William Penn's trial in 1670 allowed juries to refuse to enforce laws that they judged to be contrary to the community's moral sense.[109] In the Chinese case, as in Western pardons, the ruler's ability to halt the routine functioning of legal violence shows that his power transcended conventional legality.

Powers of adjudication were also crucial to Roman emperors' control of the empire. The rescript system, jurists and their legal expertise, precedents set by earlier emperors, and *maiestas* charges worked together to construct the power of the emperors as the supreme judges in a Roman world that had previously denounced monarchy in any form. Roman emperors became "above the law, within the law, and the law itself," and only in doing so were they able to fully become emperors.[110]

Legislative powers of emperors began under Augustus, who was given the "tribunician" power to present legislation that could become laws to the senate and popular assemblies. He also acted as the highest judge, sentencing figures such as Ovid to exile or death.[111] Subsequent emperors significantly expanded the range of their decisions through an ever more liberal interpretation of the charge of *maiestas* – that is, high treason.[112] This crime, which had originally indicated treason against the Roman people or state, was assimilated to challenges to the emperor, thus becoming a tool by which the ruler could kill anyone who displeased him.

However, the most important tool by which the Roman emperor wielded law for his own authority was the rescript system. Petitions from anyone in the empire, regardless of rank or status, were brought to emperors in the form of letters. Citing the legal advice of his judicial council, the emperor or his advisors appended a written reply below the original petition or a copy. The replies were

Schmitt's Critique of Liberalism, ed. David Dzyenhaus (Durham: Duke University Press, 1998), pp. 217–251.

[109] Daniel Heller-Roazen, *The Enemy of All: Piracy and the Law of Nations* (New York: Zone Books, 2009).

[110] Kaius Tuori, *The Emperor of Law: The Emergence of Roman Imperial Adjudication* (Oxford: Oxford University Press, 2016), p. 11. On the emperors' use of rescripts to rule (and set precedents for successors), see also Tony Honoré, *Emperors and Lawyers*, 2nd ed. rev. (Oxford: Clarendon, 1994); Jill Harries, *Law and Empire in Late Antiquity* (Cambridge: Cambridge University Press, 1999).

[111] Ovid, *The Poems of Exile: Tristia and the Black Sea Letters* (Berkeley: University of California Press, 1994), Book 2, 2, 109–20, where Ovid describes how Augustus determined his fate. On Augustus's and Tiberius's power to adjudicate, without offending the Senate, see also Tuori, *Emperor of Law*, pp. 87–88; Tacitus, *Annals*, tr. Cynthia Damon (London: Penguin Books, 2012), 3.10.

[112] Jill Harries, *Law and Crime in the Roman World* (New York: Cambridge University Press, 2007), p. 78–80; Tuori, *Emperor of Law*, p. 147.

often published together with the petitions for the public to see either in Rome or at an imperial residence. They could also be posted for viewing in provincial capitals. This system was thus a form of communication that allowed the people to bypass local courts and appeal directly to the emperor. Rescripts were originally described as only advice to local judges, but they were treated as de facto legislation. Emperors soon began to surround themselves with councils of jurists, who became the actual authors of the rescripts, and collections of these became the basis for the legal codes compiled at the end of the empire.[113] Thus both the Chinese and Roman emperors accrued authority through gaining the right to adjudicate individual cases, which became the vehicle for creating binding legal precedents.

Another instance in the early East Asian empires where routine legal functioning was often suspended was the case of vengeance. Revenge had been central to noble honor in the Spring and Autumn period, while in the Warring States and early empires it became primarily a form of serving a superior or defining family relations. Thus Yu Rang articulated the "debt" of vengeance that he owed to the man who had honored him, and it was likewise crucial to the bravoes and their networks. Most importantly, this debt of vengeance became fundamental to defining family ties in the Han. As the powerful local families became the foundation of local state power in the Eastern Han, the conventional (but not legal) endorsement of vengeance became a basic element of the regime of violence.[114]

The strongest claims for the familial obligation of vengeance, fused with the duties of retainers, came from the classicists, notably the *Gongyang Tradition*, which in the Han was the most influential commentary on the *Spring and Autumn Annals*. Noting that Zhao Dun had murdered his lord, the commentator asks why he was mentioned later, when the *Annals* never again mentioned someone who assassinated his lord. The answer explains that he was not the killer, but had failed to kill the assassin, which was tantamount to killing the lord himself. Elsewhere the text explains that the *Annals* in one case did not mention the interment of a lord, because his murderers were left unpunished, so his sons and retainers had ceased to be such. For this text, vengeance was part of the mourning duties that defined kin ties.[115]

---

[113]. Tony Honoré, *Emperors and Lawyers*, ch. 2; Tuori, *Emperor of Law*, pp. 4–6, 200–273, 284–295.

[114]. Lewis, *Sanctioned Violence*, pp. 80–94; Lewis, *Honor and Shame*, pp. 163–168; Makino Tatsumi 牧野巽, *Chūgoku kazoku kenkyū* 中國家族研究 (Tokyo: Ochanomizu, 1980), vol. 2, pp. 4–15; Bret Hinsch, *Masculinities in Chinese History* (Lanham: Rowman and Littlefield, 2013), ch. 2; Ma Zhifei, "Chunqiu Gongyang xue yu Handai fuchou fengqi fazheng 春秋公羊學與漢代復仇風氣發證," *Xuzhou Shifan Xueyuan xuebao* (*Zhexue shehui kexue ban*) (February 1996), pp. 23–28; Chen Enlin 陳恩林, "Lun Gongyang zhuan fuchou sixiang de tedian ji jin gu wen fuchoushuo wenti 論公羊傳復仇思想的特點及今古文復仇說問題," *Shehui kexue zhanxian* (February 1998), pp. 137–145.

[115]. *Gongyangzhuan zhu shu* 春秋公羊傳注疏, in *Shisan jing zhushu* 十三經注疏, vol. 7 (Taipei: Yiwen, 1976), Lord Xuan, year 2, ch. 15, p. 6b; Lord Xuan, year 6, ch. 15, pp. 10a–14b; Lord Yin, year 11, ch. 3, pp. 16b–17b. The argument that a man left unavenged has no retainer or sons also

The ritual texts also argued that avenging kin was a moral obligation, the degree of which depended on the relation to the victim.[116] Since an unavenged crime made living together impossible, these texts measured the obligation to vengeance by the distance one had to cover to pursue the offender. The *White Tiger Hall Discourses*, a record of an imperially-sponsored discussion of the classics held in 79 CE, shared this idea, while the ancient-texts classic *Rituals of Zhou* translated the distance of pursuit into a distance of exile. It also mapped kin ties onto sociopolitical ones, equating a father with a prince, a brother with a teacher, and an uncle or cousin with a master or friend.[117] The idea that the duty to avenge was based on a debt owed also explains why texts insisted on the duty of the retainer to avenge a lord or a son a father, but not the reverse. While a lord's avenging a retainer would be punishment rather than vengeance, the absence of a duty to avenge a child is best explained by the fact that fathers owed no debts to sons. Thus the duty of retainers or sons indicates how honor could be found in the subordinate position in a hierarchy, but this "diminished being" could still be marked by the necessity of performing violence.[118]

This duty of kin to act illegally elicited attempts to reconcile revenge with the state's claim to a monopoly of punishment. Thus the Eastern Han scholar, Xun Yue (148–209 CE), noted that revenge was an ancient duty, but was not always permissible. If the murderer ignored the rules of avoidance, then the avenger was free to kill him. If he observed the rules and the avenger still killed him, then the life of the latter should be forfeit. Thus Xun Yue situated the familial duty of revenge within imperial law's claims to ultimate authority.[119]

A related belief was that dead spirits could launch legal suits against the living, or other dead people. Figurines were buried in tombs to act as substitutes, which would become the targets of these suits and hence help the living avert disasters.[120]

---

appears in *Chunqiu fan lu yi zheng*春秋繁露義證, annotated by Su Yu 蘇輿 (Beijing: Zhonghua, 1992), ch. 1, sect. 2, "Yu bei," pp. 39, 42; ch. 4, sect. 6, "Wang dao," p. 117. On vengeance as a preliminary to interment, see *Shi ji*, ch. 124, pp. 3185–3186; *Hou Han shu* 後漢書, compiled by Fan Ye 范曄 (398 – 446 CE) (Beijing: Zhonghua, 1965), ch. 31, pp. 1107–1109.

116. Makino, *Chūgoku kazoku kenkyū*, vol. 2, pp. 4–15.

117. *Li ji*, ch. 3, "Qu li shang," p. 10b; ch. 7, "Tan gong shang," pp. 17a–b; *Bo hu tong de lun* 白虎通德論, compiled by Ban Gu et al., in *Han Wei congshu*, vol. 1 (Taipei: Xinxing, 1977), ch. 1, pp. 47b–48a. A variant of these formulations is in He Xiu's commentary to the *Gongyang*. See *Gongyang zhuan*, Lord Zhuang, year 4, ch. 6, p. 13b. For the *Rituals of Zhou*, see *Zhou li zhu shu* 周禮注疏, in *Shisan jing zhu shu*, vol. 3 (Taipei: Yiwen, 1976), ch. 14, "Tiao ren," pp. 10b–13a.

118. On the hidden power of sons, see Lewis, *Flood Myths of Early China* (Albany: SUNY Press, 2006), pp. 95–106; Angela Zito, *Of Body and Brush: Grand Sacrifice as Text/Performance in Eighteenth-Century China* (Chicago: University of Chicago Press, 1997), pp. 202–206.

119. Xun Yue, *Shen jian*, ch. 2, pp. 6a–7a.

120. Anna Seidel, "Geleitbrief an die Unterwelt: Jenseitsvorstellungen in den Graburkunden der späteren Han Zeit," in *Religion und Philosophie in Ostasien: Festschrift für Hans Steininger*, ed. Gert Naundorf, Karl-Heinz Pohl, and Hans-Hermann Schmidt (Würzburg: Königshausen und Neumann, 1985), pp. 166–171; Mu-chou Poo, *In Search of Personal Welfare* (Albany: SUNY Press, 1998), pp. 167–175; Lewis, *Construction of Space*, pp. 122–125.

These show how living kin were entangled in legal attacks on deceased relatives, a form of entanglement that followed the pattern marked by obligations of vengeance. However, it also dramatizes the tension between legal forms, in this case the laws enforced by Heaven, and the debts that kin owed one another.

Despite their court bias, Han historical records also document frequent popular recourse to revenge. Makino Tatsumi collected from Han histories more than sixty cases of murder or attempted murder described as vengeance. Bravoes served as hired avengers, so Sima Qian listed vengeance as something people did for money.[121] A memorial by Bao Xuan (d. 3 CE) listed the major causes of unnatural deaths and, along with rapacious officials, bandits, plagues, and famine, he included reciprocal slaughter due to vengeance. Huan Tan (24 BCE–56 CE) told the Eastern Han founder that vengeance was so common and so admired that it formed a private legal system. Another writer explained the prevalence of vengeance as the lingering influence of the Four Princes that still guided bravoes, as well as the violent foundation of the Han and the dominance of military men in its first century.[122] Here all the forms of licit violence that had defined the Western Han "hierarchy of being" were drawn together, but they served to justify to some degree the emerging power of the great families within the evolving imperial order.

Despite these worries over vengeance as privatized law, many officials refused to arrest those guilty of such murders. Some released those already arrested, and although the officials sometimes had to go into hiding, many continued in office. Officials even honored avengers with privileges, such as exemption from corvée, or recommended them for office. Both these officials and the authors of the histories described avengers as models of "duty," and some officials honored avengers by erecting illustrated memorial tablets celebrating them as exemplars of filial piety. Briefly in the Eastern Han, releasing avengers came to be regarded as a fixed legal precedent, which was reinstituted under the Wei dynasty (220–265 CE).[123]

However, honoring avengers was not automatic. As Jen-der Lee has shown, officials were torn between commitment to kin ties that demanded private blood justice and to the rule of law. Her statistical examination shows that Han officials never resolved their ambivalence, with each acting as he saw fit.[124] Lee describes this as a conflict between "legal authority" and "ethical ideals."

[121.] For Sima Qian's list of the activities that people do for money, see *Shi ji*, ch. 129, p. 3271. For examples of paid avengers and assassins, see Lewis, *Sanctioned Violence*, ch. 2, note 137.

[122.] *Han shu*, ch. 72, p. 3088; *Hou Han shu*, ch. 28a, p. 958; ch. 67, p. 2184.

[123.] Lewis, *Sanctioned Violence*, ch. 2, n. 142–147.

[124.] Jen-der Lee, "Conflicts and Compromise between Legal Authority and Ethical Ideas: From the Perspective of Revenge in Han Times," *Renwen ji shehui kexue jikan* 1:1 (1988), pp. 359–408.

However, publicly celebrating kin ties became fundamental to the Han government, so honoring avengers was as much an expression of government authority (although not "legal") as was the decision to punish them. This again shows how the hierarchies defined through the regime of violence and that of formal, legal structures would often diverge, or be in permanent, irreconcilable tension. This was as true of the "centralized" empire as it had been among the Zhou nobility, and between the Warring States.

Celebrating revenge was not limited to the textually sanctioned avenging of slain kin; avenging affronts to honor also gained glory:

> When young [Ji Zun] loved the classics. His family was rich, but he was respectful and frugal, disliking fine clothing. His mother died, so he piled up earth for her tomb. Previously he had been bullied by a local clerk, so he gathered retainers and killed him. At first the people of his district had regarded him as weak, but after this act they held him in awe.[125]

Perhaps fearing that his mother might suffer legal repercussions, he waited until she was buried before avenging himself. The response of the local people shows that commoners admired men who used violence to defend their honor. He even received an appointment as a district clerk, and was later presented to Emperor Guangwu, who admired his bearing and appointed him as a scribe. He again proved his heroism by executing a man of whom Guangwu was fond, which led to a promotion and ultimately enfeoffment. Thus even emperors justified some uses of illegal violence, here in the service of personal honor.

Another case was that of Yang Qiu:

> His family for generations had been among the leading great surnames. Qiu was a skillful swordsman, practiced in archery and riding a horse, and by nature very fierce. He loved the teachings of Shen Buhai and Han Fei. Among the clerks in the commandery was one who insulted his mother, so Qiu gathered several dozen youths, killed the clerk, and wiped out his family. From this he became famous . . . and was appointed a gentleman-attendant in the Secretariat.[126]

Yang was violent and skilled in weaponry, the provocation was an insult to his *mother* (who was often the center of the Eastern Han family), and the murder resulted in his receiving his first official appointment. This again shows the divergence between formal law and the actual order created through forms of violence sanctioned by popular ideas.[127]

Socially endorsed vengeance could even be done for friends:

[125.] *Hou Han shu*, ch. 20, p. 738–739.   [126.] *Hou Han shu*, ch. 77, p. 2498.

[127.] On the increasing power and prestige of mothers in the Eastern Han, see Lewis, *Honor and Shame*, pp. 171–180, 184–185.

Zhongqing avenged a friend to fulfill his duty in accord with reason [*li* 理].

> Chen Gang, whose cognomen was Zhongqing, was a man of Chengu. When young he studied at Nanyang with Zhang Zong, who came from the same commandery. Because of his mother's death he returned home for the funeral. Zong was killed by Liu Yuan of Anzhong. When Gang had finished mourning his mother, he went to seek vengeance. He found Yuan drunk and asleep, so he went back to his own dwelling, waited for him to wake up, and only then killed him. He then surrendered to the authorities. An empire-wide pardon occurred, so he was released ... He was recommended as a Flourishing Talent, and then appointed the grand commandant of Hongnong.[128]

This politically endorsed murder of a friend's killer, which received the blessing of a general pardon, was also celebrated for the thoughtful and proper manner of its execution.

In the Introduction I noted that centralized states in this period in East Asia, like the earlier polities, did not claim a "monopoly" of violence as used in Weber's definition of the state. This discussion of vengeance has highlighted one aspect of the phenomenon. While vengeance was illegal, it was also normative; the agents of the imperial state remained perpetually divided over how to deal with it, and emperors often honored it. To the extent that the powerful local families had emerged as the foundation of the Eastern Han state, in contrast with previous states that had based themselves on individual peasant households paying taxes and providing service, this endorsement of vengeance was a form of recognizing powerful families, and more broadly their local networks, as elements of the imperial order. This practice was facilitated by the endorsement of vengeance as an expression of kin solidarity that had been articulated in the classics, their commentaries, and Han adaptations of the classics such as the *Zhou li*.

In addition to the recognition of vengeance as a normative form of violence wielded outside the state, there were at least seven other ways in which violence that potentially served public order was pursued outside formal channels. First, it was generally recognized that dynastic states had to be established through the violent overthrow of the preceding dynasty, an action which was criminal in its origins and only validated through a "Mandate" from Heaven which provided a post facto religious sanction for any successful rebellion.[129] This was

---

[128.] Chang Qu 常璩 (fl. CE 347), *Huayang guo zhi jiao zhu* 華陽國志校注, annotated by Liu Lin 劉琳 (Taipei: Xin Wen Feng, 1988), ch. 10c, p. 570.

[129.] This idea was also acknowledged in the West, as in Sir John Harrington's poetic observation, "Treason doth never prosper, what's the reason? For if it prosper none dare call it treason." It is also implicit in Barfield's argument that the seminomadic peoples of the northeast who conquered China – from the Xianbei through the Manchus – differed from steppe tribes (Xiongnu, Turks, etc.) because the former combined foreign military conquerors with Hua

articulated in the *Han Feizi* and the *Zhuangzi*, which argued that the Shang and Zhou founders were criminals like any other rebels; the *Zhuangzi*, which noted that if you stole a belt buckle they would execute you, but if you stole a state you became ruler; and later in the idea that the obedience of imperial subjects served as ropes by which bandit conquerors carried off loot.[130]

Second, while dynastic states rose through illicit violence, or violence rendered licit only after the fact, even in times of peace and order the violent potential that could re-create the political order lay constantly present. For example, the bravoes and their networks provided a pool of violent men who could be recruited. In addition to those who were effectively gangsters, some men of good social background also acted as bravoes due to a martial temperament or for entertainment. Allies of the Han founder or Xiang Yu followed the pattern noted by Sima Qian of bravoes who in times of disorder became political actors.[131] Other elites – even members of the imperial family – won renown through heroic conduct, gathering followers who served them to the death. Some local families had a history of disturbing social order, and whole areas had violent traditions. Other great families, such as the Dou, had a tradition of acting as bravoes, thereby winning fame that enabled them to become officials. Many were noted for their contempt for material wealth and their consequent generosity. The "cruel clerks" also sometimes acted as bravoes, so that their networks (technically criminal) served the functioning of the Han state.[132]

---

bureaucrats who administered the conquered populace. This pattern of conquerors establishing their rule through force, while incorporating conquered elites to administer on their behalf, was true of *all* East Asian empires, not just "conquest dynasties." See Thomas J. Barfield, *The Perilous Frontier: Nomadic Empires and China* (Cambridge, MA: Blackwell, 1989), ch. 3.

[130.] *Han Feizi ji shi*, ch. 17, "Shuo yi," p. 925–926; *Zhuangzi ji shi* 莊子集釋, in *Xin bian zhuzi ji cheng*, vol. 3 (Taipei: Shijie, 1974), ch. 11, "Qu jie," p. 159; ch. 17, "Qiu shui," p. 256; ch. 29. "Dao Zhi," pp. 429–430, 430–431, 434 (2).

[131.] See also the biography of Cao Cao (ca. 155–220 CE), who "acted as a bravo, behaved wildly, and did not devote himself to any business." One observer told him: "In a time of order you would be a capable minister, but in times of chaos you will be a treacherous hero." See *San guo zhi* 三國志, compiled by Chen Shou 陳壽 (233–297) (Beijing: Zhonghua, 1959), ch. 1, p. 2.

[132.] *Shi ji*, ch. 49, p. 1974; ch. 55, p. 2036; ch. 100, p. 2729 (Ji Bu became famous as a bravo), p. 2732 (Bu's younger brother as a bravo won followers who served him to the death); ch. 107, p. 2847 (Guan Fu forged a network of eminent friends, local bosses, and bravoes); ch. 118, p. 3090; ch. 120, p. 3112; ch. 122, p. 3135; *Han shu*, ch. 28b, p. 1642 (in the Qin region bold people acted as bravoes and joined with criminals), p. 1665; ch. 69, p. 2998 (a son of a general and an uncle of the young Emperor Ping wandered about as bravoes and gathered many retainers); ch. 100b, p. 4198 (the local community sings songs about an ancestor of Ban Gu who acted as a bravo); *Hou Han shu*, ch. 9, p. 370; ch. 12, p. 491 (local heroes gathered around a member of the imperial family who acted as a bravo); ch. 23, p. 795; ch. 30b, p. 1075; ch. 31, p. 1091 (the son and grandson of a celebrated bravo under Emperor Wu rose to be high officials); ch. 42, p. 1428 (a young Eastern Han king, who later became one of the first converts to Buddhism, loved bravoes and gathered retainers); ch. 55, p. 1798 (in late Eastern Han, a frustrated prince linked up in rebellion with officials who acted as bravoes); ch. 72, p. 2328.

Networks uniting bravoes and officials, or the fluid boundary between these two groups, also were criticized in discussions of vengeance, as in accounts of associations of professional assassins who joined with officials in the capital.[133] However, the blurred line between bravoes and officials could have benefits, as in this account of Emperor Xuan in his youth:

> He had great talent and loved to study, but he also delighted in [the company of] wandering bravoes, participating in cockfights and horse races. He came to know all the treachery and deviance in the side streets and alleys of the capital, and was completely familiar with the successes and failures of local officials.[134]

His acquaintance with bravoes allowed him to observe actual local administration in the capital, equipping him to later be a better emperor.

Third, while in peace these networks remained in the background (or underground) of the Han state, in times of breakdown they became major sources of armed supporters. Accounts of assembling forces to resist Wang Mang or topple the Eastern Han demonstrate such men's willingness to swear devotion to the death to political patrons.[135] The values of these local stalwarts were shared by political actors, who pardoned men who displayed loyalty to their defeated rivals, or honored them with offices. Bandits also honored such men.[136] Thus these networks, which were permanent aspects of Han society, became fundamental to later dynastic transitions, as in the groups trained in martial arts who were crucial to the rebel armies at the fall of the Tang.

A fourth aspect of this violence hidden in the imperial order that emerged only at times of dynastic transition was the role of nomadic peoples at the frontier. From the Eastern Han on, as already discussed, nomads who were resettled inside the frontiers could become crucial to the armies of rebels in the north. Moreover, nomadic or seminomadic states in the north were permanent parts of the political order, without being subjects of whatever dynasty was in power in the Yellow River valley and the Yangzi. As in the case of the Han, these outside threats (here the Xiongnu) served to elevate the position of emperor through his unique relations to them, potentially marked by the exchange of gifts, or to justify claims for the necessity of a strong, active emperor to engage them in war. Finally, in the post-Han world such people frequently established their authority over the north, or in a handful of cases over the entire East Asian subcontinent. While such conquest could never be

---

[133.] *Han shu*, ch. 90, pp. 3673–3674; *Qian fu lun*, ch. 5, p. 183.   [134.] *Han shu*, ch. 8, p. 237.

[135.] *Hou Han shu*, ch. 13, pp. 522, 533, 534; ch. 21, pp. 760, 761. This last also refers to them as "retainers." On such "retainers" in the armed opposition to Wang Mang and the warlord armies at the end of the Han, see Lewis, *Construction of Space*, pp. 219–224.

[136.] *Hou Han shu*, 11, p. 486; ch. 14, p. 533; ch. 17, pp. 653, 654; ch. 19, p. 1020; ch. 39, p. 1296; ch. 8a, pp. 2673, 2676.

completely acknowledged as routine, it was in fact simply a version of any possible dynastic foundation, and over the course of East Asian history was crucial to the pattern of constant reunification that distinguished its history from that of the West.

A fifth aspect of licit violence granted to nonstate actors was the recognition of parents' rights, particularly those of fathers, to forcibly chastise offspring. Because the Qin code gave legal sanction to the authority of parents, a son's denunciation of his father could not be accepted as evidence, and the denouncer could be punished for making the accusation. The father could use the legal system to punish his children, even banishing or executing them. Routine, low-level violence of fathers against children in the name of discipline also seems to have been the norm. Wang Chong's first-century CE autobiography notes how remarkable it was that his father never flogged him. Later writing shows that such beatings were a regular aspect of education in China for over two millennia.[137] Of course, such familial violence is also often permitted in modern, Western states, where a husband might be permitted to rape or beat his wife, or kill her and a lover if he caught them in flagrante.

A sixth form of dispersed licit violence was sacrifice. In the Warring States and early empires, authority in every social unit was marked by the power to offer victims to the spirits of that unit. Thus at the beginning of the Han, the emperor sacrificed to various powerful spirits, and at the end of the Western Han offerings to Heaven were established as the central rituals of empire, with a capital defined by the presence of an altar to Heaven as the core of a ritual complex in the southern suburbs.[138] Similarly, local officials handled sacrifices to the deities of nature in the areas they administered, and leaders of local communities often conducted sacrifices to local mountains or rivers that were not listed in the state registers.[139] Finally, heads of households sacrificed to the spirits of their ancestors. Thus the dispersal of the right to sacrifice marked a more general dispersal of authority, with the state constituting the pinnacle of a broader range of powers, but accepting the de facto authority of the heads of local communities and families.

[137.] Lewis, *Early Chinese Empires*, p. 232.

[138.] On sacrifice as violence that created authority in the Warring States and early empires, see index of Lewis, *Sanctioned Violence*, under "sacrifice." On imperial sacrifices at the beginning of the empires, see Lewis, "The *Feng* and *Shan* Sacrifices of Emperor Wu of the Han," in *State and Court Ritual in China*, ed. Joseph McDermott (Cambridge: Cambridge University Press, 1999), pp. 50–80. On the establishment of the cult of Heaven as the central imperial ritual and defining feature of the capital, see Lewis, *Early Chinese Empires*, pp. 88–101, 185–189; Marianne Bujard, *Le Sacrifice au Ciel dans la Chine ancienne: Théorie et pratique sous les Han occidentaux* (Paris: École Française d'Extrême-Orient, 2000).

[139.] Kenneth Brashier, "The Spirit Lord of Baishi Mountain: Feeding the Deities or Heeding the Yinyang?" *Early China* 26–27 (2001–2002): 159–231.

A final violent activity, also taking the form of violence against animals, was hunting. As discussed earlier, hunting under the Shang had been a form of military action which served to generate royal power, and hunts down through the Eastern Zhou had remained a military ritual in which the army was assembled and, when necessary, state power restructured.[140] In the Western Han, the Shanglin hunting park became a major ritual site of empire, and the great hunts conducted there were celebrated in the most famous pieces of poetry composed in the era, the rhapsodies on the hunt by Sima Xiangru and later Yang Xiong. While we have less evidence on hunts among the elite, scenes of hunting and staged animal combats figure in the art of Eastern Han elite tombs. Moreover, the rhapsodies on the capitals of Shu and Wu, composed by Zuo Si a couple of generations after the Han, described hunts by local elites rather than by the emperor.[141] Such hunts almost certainly existed in the Eastern Han, but they were not yet suitable topics for writing.

Conclusion

At every stage of the evolution of political power in East Asia, those in power relied on violence to generate the hierarchy from which they benefited. Through war, hunting, and sacrifice, and later wielding more articulated and measurable forms of violence such as law, they diminished those around them to the ranked levels of obedient followers, deviants to be expelled or exploited, enemies to be conquered, nameless "political capital" to be sacrificed, or the equivalent of beasts. However, the power thus generated could not be fully domesticated, articulated, or measured, and hence could never be entirely suited to the tasks of administration or control. Thus in the Shang those closest to the king might (through an unclear procedure) be selected as "death attendants," while the lines between followers, allies, and enemies constantly shifted. In the Eastern Zhou, the nobles' commitment to an honor based on violence challenged the kin structure, producing endless wars, civil wars, vendettas, and assassinations, in which killing the ruler could "perfect one's fame." While the elective ties that created the Warring States escaped this contradiction through adopting the ideal of the retainers' "devotion to the death," this very ideal justified leading officials in assembling followers and private armies who challenged the monarch, and peasant armies gathered and ranked through the new systems of law and administration were devoted to the destruction of states and mass slaughter.

[140.] On hunting as a military and political activity, and an imperial ritual, see also index of Lewis, *Sanctioned Violence*, under "hunting"; Lewis, *Honor and Shame*, pp. 24–26.

[141.] Lewis, *Sanctioned Violence*, pp. 150–160; Lewis, *China Between Empires: The Northern and Southern Dynasties* (Cambridge, MA: Belknap Press of Harvard University, 2009), pp. 89–91.

The united empire ultimately abolished such armies, but consequently was forced to rely on tribesmen who remained loyal to their chieftains, professional armies that were the creatures of their commanders, powerful families who ruled their regions with militarized followers, and ultimately alien conquerors who became the primary mechanism of creating unified states. Law seemed to be a tool of civilized control, just in its procedures and measurable in its punishments, but it ultimately hinged on the power of the supreme autocrats, who were both lawgivers and supreme judges. This was highlighted in the different legal treatments applied to special groups. Ordinary people passed through routine legal procedures as modified by their ranks, and were subject to the full range of punishments. Officials came to be set apart as a "privileged" group who were allowed to commit suicide, an act of imperial grace, rather than suffer the humiliation of mutilation and exposure. Powerful families were sometimes subjected to unique treatment, with legal texts being manipulated to destroy them and confiscate their wealth on behalf of the emperor. Finally, the emperors relied on the service of eunuchs who suffered punishments to gain privilege and power. Moreover, emperors regularly suspended the routine function of law by granting amnesties and pardons. In the emperor's role as supreme judge (a role justified by his power to judge the most honored and powerful), the emperor's word became law through decisions in specific cases. The imperial legal order was also more or less permanently suspended through the widespread recognition of vengeance, technically illegal, as supremely filial and honored in local communities, by which it served to endorse powerful families as the basis of the state.

Finally, all empires were based on the post facto recognition of rebellion or conquest, which until the moment of victory were criminal violations of the imperial order. While such events were infrequent, numerous groups – gangs of bravoes, officials and elites who linked themselves with such men, resettled nomads, frontier garrisons, and powerful families – formed a permanent world of latent violence that both participated in the public order and challenged it through their extralegal violence. Thus, from the first emergence of political forms through the establishment of the centralized, universal empire as the ideal model, violence remained both fundamental to the social order, and a destructive force that permanently divided it against itself.

Cambridge Elements ≡

Elements in Ancient East Asia

Erica Fox Brindley
Pennsylvania State University

Erica Fox Brindley is Professor and Head in the Department of Asian Studies at Pennsylvania State University. She is the author of three books, co-editor of several volumes, and the recipient of the ACLS Ryskamp Fellowship and Humboldt Fellowship. Her research focuses on the history of the self, knowledge, music, and identity in ancient China, as well as on the history of the Yue/Viet cultures from southern China and Vietnam.

Rowan Kimon Flad
Harvard University

Rowan Kimon Flad is the John E. Hudson Professor of Archaeology in the Department of Anthropology at Harvard University. He has authored two books and over 50 articles, edited several volumes, and served as editor of *Asian Perspectives*. His archaeological research focuses on economic and ritual activity, interregional interaction, and technological and environmental change, in the late Neolithic and early Bronze Ages of the Sichuan Basin and the Upper Yellow River valley regions of China.

About the Series

Elements in Ancient East Asia contains multi-disciplinary contributions focusing on the history and culture of East Asia in ancient times. Its framework extends beyond anachronistic, nation-based conceptions of the past, following instead the contours of Asian sub-regions and their interconnections with each other. Within the series there are five thematic groups: 'Sources', which includes excavated texts and other new sources of data; 'Environments', exploring interaction zones of ancient East Asia and long-distance connections; 'Institutions', including the state and its military; 'People', including family, gender, class, and the individual and 'Ideas', concerning religion and philosophy, as well as the arts and sciences. The series presents the latest findings and strikingly new perspectives on the ancient world in East Asia.

Cambridge Elements $\equiv$

Elements in Ancient East Asia

Elements in the Series

Violence and the Rise of Centralized States in East Asia
Mark Edward Lewis

A full series listing is available at: www.cambridge.org/ECTP

Printed in the United States
by Baker & Taylor Publisher Services